MW01233677

THE NO-NONSENSE ANXIOUS ATTACHMENT BOOK

BECOME SECURE IN LIFE, DATING, LOVE, RELATIONSHIPS, AND WORK THROUGH COGNITIVE BEHAVIORAL THERAPY, SELF-CARE, AND TARGETED TECHNIQUES

JEFFREY C. CHAPMAN

© Copyright 2023 - Jeffrey C. Chapman. All rights reserved.

The content contained within this book may not be reproduced, duplicated or transmitted without direct written permission from the author or the publisher.

Under no circumstances will any blame or legal responsibility be held against the publisher, or author, for any damages, reparation, or monetary loss due to the information contained within this book, either directly or indirectly.

Legal Notice:

This book is copyright protected. It is only for personal use. You cannot amend, distribute, sell, use, quote or paraphrase any part, or the content within this book, without the consent of the author or publisher.

Disclaimer Notice:

Please note the information contained within this document is for educational and entertainment purposes only. All effort has been executed to present accurate, up to date, reliable, complete information. No warranties of any kind are declared or implied. Readers acknowledge that the author is not engaged in the rendering of legal, financial, medical or professional advice. The content within this book has been derived from various sources. Please consult a licensed professional before attempting any techniques outlined in this book.

By reading this document, the reader agrees that under no circumstances is the author responsible for any losses, direct or indirect, that are incurred as a result of the use of the information contained within this document, including, but not limited to, errors, omissions, or inaccuracies.

DISCLAIMER

The contents of this book, including the exercises, techniques, and insights provided, are intended for educational and self-help purposes only. The author of this book is not a licensed mental health professional, medical practitioner, or therapist, and the information presented should not be construed as professional medical or psychological advice.

The strategies and suggestions found within these pages are based on the author's personal experience, research, and general understanding of anxious attachment and related subjects. They are not meant to diagnose, treat, or cure any medical or mental health condition.

Readers who are dealing with mental health challenges or who have specific concerns related to anxious attachment or any other emotional or psychological issues are strongly encouraged to seek the guidance of qualified mental health professionals.

The author and publisher have made every effort to ensure the accuracy and completeness of the information contained in this book but assume no responsibility for errors, inaccuracies, omissions, or any inconsistency herein. The reader assumes all risks and responsibilities for their use of the materials and information within this book.

Please consult with a healthcare provider if you need professional assistance with any health-related or mental health concerns.

CONTENTS

INTRODUCTION

Even though I was with friends at a party, I can still remember that feeling of worry. Was I saying the right thing? Was I too excited or not excited enough? My thoughts were racing, and even when I was with friends, a cloud of worry hung over me. A quick look at a friend's worried face across the room or the warmth of a stranger's encouraging smile were small things that either calmed me down or made me more worried.

Many people can relate to that feeling of worry, insecurity, and, in some cases, a deep fear of being abandoned. But this isn't just about me or a small group of people. It is an experience that goes beyond borders, cultures, and individual pasts. It's the perfect example of a complicated mental condition called "anxious attachment."

Think about Sarah, a young, active woman in her thirties who is in a loving relationship but stays up at night worrying that her partner will leave. Or think about Tom, a hard worker who can't get rid of the idea that his coworkers might not like what he does. There are echoes of anxious attachment everywhere, from the playgrounds of childhood to the complicated web of adult relationships.

Why do we want to talk about this topic? Maybe it's because in a world full of connections, both online and off, feeling alone and being afraid of being left behind is more common than ever. It's a theme that moves through relationships and personal well-being, giving them shades of worry, dependence, and sometimes even despair.

We'll learn about the fascinating world of anxious attachment through this tapestry of words and wisdom. A topic that is not only important in today's world but also a must-know. Through the lens of existing literature and with the goal of shedding light on the unseen, this book takes the reader on a journey into areas that are often not talked about.

This is not a scientific analysis, but a heartfelt look at something. It gives you a chance to put yourself in the shoes of someone with anxious attachment and learn about their world, their fears, and their hopes. We'll meet moms, dads, lovers, and friends, all of whom have their own way of dancing with anxious attachment.

Together, we'll peel back the layers of science and emotion, look at the effects on relationships and ourselves, and give ourselves tools and strategies to help us navigate the rough seas of anxious attachment. We'll listen to the stories, share the tears and laughter, and grow in our ability to understand and care about each other.

Here is a gift of understanding, sympathy, and kindness. A hand reaches out to you, inviting you to join me on this journey. This book has something for everyone, whether you have anxious attachment yourself, know someone who does, or are just interested in how people live.

So get a warm blanket and a cup of your favorite drink and settle in. The world of anxious attachment is waiting for you, and I'm honored to be your guide on this deeply personal and universally relevant journey.

Definition of Anxious Attachment

Imagine a child holding a parent's hand tightly, with wide eyes and fear in their faces at the thought of letting go. This image, which is simple but still powerful, starts to show how complicated anxious attachment is.

Anxious attachment is not just a word; it is a real, living thing. It's like a song that plays in the background of some people's lives, a song of longing, fear, and an unquenchable need for reassurance.

At its core, anxious attachment is a way of being in a relationship that is marked by a constant fear that love and connection will be taken away. Imagine a friend who is always checking their phone for texts from their partner. Every reassuring text makes them feel better, but they are never really at ease.

From early bonds with caregivers to romantic relationships in adulthood, anxious attachment creates a pattern of dependence, doubt, and fear of being left alone. It's the voice that asks, "Are you sure they love you?" It's the feeling you get when someone you care about calls a little late. It's the nights you can't sleep because you're not sure if you're really seen, valued, and loved.

Think of it as a dance where the steps are uncertain and the music is a haunting version of "What if?" It's a dance full of longing and uncertainty that can be both beautiful and painful.

Anxious attachment is not a mistake or a flaw; it's a way of interacting with the world. It's part of how people connect and disconnect with each other, a thread in the complex web of relationships.

As we go deeper into this book, we'll look at this idea from different points of view to find out where it came from, how it shows up in the world, and how it affects our lives. But for now, just know that anxious attachment is not a far-off, vague concept. It is a real part of life that is often misunderstood. Many people go on this journey to find understanding, compassion, and ultimately healing.

· · · ● · ● · · ·

Why is this Subject Relevant and Important?

We live in a time when we can connect with just a swipe of our finger, when "friends" are counted in numbers, and when "likes" are sought after like precious gems. This is an ironic twist of fate. We're more connected, but also more alone, involved, but not really involved, and together, but alone. It's a paradox that helps us understand our emotions, especially when it comes to anxious attachment.

You might wonder why we should get involved in this complicated world of anxious attachment. What does it mean, and why should we pay attention to it?

Let's take a walk down a busy city street where everyone is looking at their phones. Lisa is one of them. She is a young professional who finds comfort in the virtual praise she gets on social media, but in her real-life relationships, she struggles with a fear of being left alone. Her story is just a drop in the ocean of anxious attachment, which affects a huge number of people in different ways.

Attachment anxiety isn't limited to romantic relationships or family ties. It affects our friendships, our jobs, how we raise our kids, and even how we treat ourselves. It doesn't only matter to people of a certain age, gender, or culture; it's a universal human experience that shows how much we want to connect with others and how afraid we are of being unlovable.

Understanding anxious attachment is more than just a matter of academic interest. It's about recognizing a silent cry for connection in a world that often leaves us alone. It's about having empathy, compassion, and the wisdom to see what's really going on between people.

In schools, knowing about anxious attachment can help teachers help kids who may feel unsafe or too dependent. Seeing the signs at work can lead to a more caring and understanding environment. In our personal lives, this knowledge can change relationships and give us a more compassionate way to look at ourselves and other people.

Exploring anxious attachment is a way to heal and grow, which may be the most important thing about it. By recognizing this part of our emotional selves, we open the door to self-awareness, acceptance, and the chance to make more secure and satisfying connections.

In the pages that follow, we'll not only break down the idea of "anxious attachment," but also look at what it means to be human. We'll hear the stories, feel the feelings, and get the tools we need to get through this complicated but deeply human experience.

So, when we turn the page to talk about the science, the effects, and the healing, know that you are starting on a journey that echoes the heartbeat of our times. Anxious attachment isn't just a footnote in the history of psychology; it's a chapter in the story of what it means to love, fear, hope, and connect in a world that's always changing but always human.

Overview of Existing Literature

The winding path to understanding anxious attachment is not a road that few people take. Scholars, therapists, authors, and people with curious minds have walked these trails, leaving behind a rich landscape of thoughts, studies, and insights. The research that has been done on anxious attachment is like a mosaic, with each piece adding to a fuller picture of what it means to have this kind of connection.

In the beginning, attachment theory was built on the work of John Bowlby[1], a psychologist who did some of the most important research on the subject in the middle of the 20th century. His work made people realize how important a child's relationship with their caretakers is and how these early experiences can shape our relationships as adults. Bowlby's ideas are still being used in research today, which shows how important they are.

Mary Ainsworth[2] took Bowlby's lead and shared the "Strange Situation" study with the world. Her observations helped us learn about different types of attachment, such as anxious attachment. This important work started a conversation that has lasted for many years and continues to shape both clinical practice and people's everyday ideas about relationships.

In the past few years, the field of anxious attachment has grown to look at how social changes, like the rise of social media and the changing nature of modern relationships, affect people. Scholars like Dr. Sherry Turkle[3] have studied how technology changes the way we connect with each other and how this may cause or worsen attachment anxiety.

---

1. Bowlby, John (1983). Attachment: Attachment and Loss Volume One (Basic Books Classics)

2. Ainsworth, M. D. (1964). Patterns of attachment behavior shown by the infant in interaction with his mother. Merrill-Palmer Quarterly of behavior and Development, 51-58.

3. Turkle, Sherry (2017). Alone Together. Basic Books; 3rd edition

Literature about therapy and ways to get better has also grown. From mindfulness practices to cognitive-behavioral techniques, authors and mental health professionals offer a wide range of tools to help people with anxious attachment deal with its many challenges. Both Dr. Sue Johnson[4], who wrote about emotionally focused therapy, and Dr. Daniel Siegel[5], who wrote about mindfulness, have made important contributions to this field, which is growing all the time.

Even books of fiction and autobiographies have talked about this subject. Writers have written heartfelt stories about their own experiences with anxious attachment and wove them into stories that people from all walks of life can relate to.

Literature about anxious attachment is neither dry nor uncaring. Instead, it is a lively, multifaceted look at how complicated human emotions are. Theories, practices, and stories all come together to make a tapestry that is both rich and informative.

In this book, we'll explore some of these places with the help of the knowledge of those who have been there before. We'll also make new paths with the help of real-life stories and useful tips. Together, we'll add our voices to this ongoing conversation and help people understand something that is so fundamentally human but is often misunderstood.

As we go deeper into the world of anxious attachment, we will learn from scholars, therapists, writers, and regular people. They help us find our way, and each one adds a different color to our understanding and appreciation of this complicated, interesting, and very important part of how people connect with each other.

· • ● ● • ● ● ● ·

4. Johnson, Sue (2019). Attachment Theory in Practice: Emotionally Focused Therapy (EFT) with Individuals, Couples, and Families. The Guilford Press

5. Siegel, Daniel (2010). Mindsight, The New Science of Personal Transformation. Random House Publishing Group.

Purpose and Structure of this Book

Let me take off my academic hat for a moment and talk to you as a fellow traveler on this interesting and enlightening journey. You might be asking, "Why this book?" What makes it different, and what do we hope to accomplish?

The goal of this book is like opening a hidden door that leads to understanding, empathy, healing, and most of all, connection. It's not just an explanation of what anxious attachment is; it's also a no-nonsense guide to understanding why it happens and how to deal with it.

We want to make theories and studies more real by turning them into things you can hold, feel, and use in your own life. We're not here to teach but to talk, tell stories, listen, and learn.

We'll go into uncharted areas of the human heart and mind, looking for not just answers but also wisdom. We'll look into the science without losing sight of what's important. We'll talk about therapies, but we won't forget the importance of the human touch. We'll go into the personal, but we won't lose sight of the big picture.

Here's what we're going to do:

Part I: Understanding Anxious Attachment will lay the groundwork by looking at where anxious attachment comes from, how it shows up, and how complicated it is. It will be the basis for the rest of what we learn.

Part II: Navigating Relationships with Anxious Attachment will be your map in the wilderness of human connections. Whether it's about love, friendship, being a parent, or the way things work at work, we'll give you tips and advice to help you find your way.

Part III: Coping Mechanisms and Healing Strategies will be like a caring friend who gives you useful advice, tips, and techniques to help you grow, heal, and thrive.

Part IV, "Support and Resources," is your toolbox. It has advice, resources, and steps you can take to help you or someone you care about understand and heal.

We will break up our discussion of the topic with real-life stories, anecdotes, and personal thoughts. There won't be any boring lectures here. Instead, you can expect interesting conversations, heartfelt insights, and maybe even a few laughs.

Consider this book your travel guide, companion, and friend on a journey to understand something that is deeply human, often painful, but always full of opportunities for growth and connection.

Let's look at the landscape of anxious attachment together, keeping our eyes and hearts open to new information and compassion. Let's go on a journey not just of the mind but also of the soul. By learning about anxious attachment, we'll understand ourselves and each other better. Shall we begin?

CHAPTER ONE

PART I: UNDERSTANDING ANXIOUS ATTACHMENT

The Science of Anxious Attachment. It sounds like the title of a science fiction book or a complicated theory, but it's neither. It's a deep and detailed look at a phenomenon that's been around as long as people have, but that we're still trying to figure out.

Imagine a newborn baby reaching for its mother with wide eyes and grabbing fingers. This instinctual need to connect with others starts as soon as we are born and shapes how we interact with the world.

But what happens when this model isn't right? When instead of warmth, there's uncertainty; instead of safety, there's anxiety? That's where the science of anxious attachment begins.

Anxious attachment is like a dance where the steps are out of sync. It's a desire for closeness mixed with a fear of being turned down. It's not just a personality quirk; it's a complicated mix of biology, psychology, and life experience.

The science of anxious attachment is a journey into the very nature of how people connect with each other. Like any great journey, it has been led by some of the brightest minds in the world. It's not just a theoretical project; it's an investigation that walks the thin line between science and emotion, where biology meets empathy and theories are mixed with real-life experiences.

Let's start with John Bowlby, who is considered the father of attachment theory. In the middle of the 20th century, Bowlby's work gave us a look into the lives of babies and the people who cared for them. It showed how these early relationships shape a child's emotional personality. His observations helped us figure out how attachment patterns, like anxious attachment, develop.

Mary Ainsworth, who was one of Bowlby's students and worked with him, added to this understanding with her "Strange Situation" study[1] . She was the first person to classify attachment styles in a clear way. For example, she was the first person to talk about anxious attachment as a separate pattern. Her work illuminated how a child's response to separation and reunion with their caregiver could be a window into their inner emotional world.

More recently, neuroscientists like Dr. Allan Schore have looked into how our brains are built and how they work to learn more about anxious attachment. Schore and others have shown through brain imaging and in-depth psychological studies how our early experiences not only shape our emotions but also change our brains. They've shown us that patterns like anxious attachment aren't just personality quirks, but are built into our bodies.

Dr. Sue Johnson, a major supporter of Emotionally Focused Therapy[2] , has looked into how anxious attachment affects relationships between adults. Her methods of therapy have been a lighthouse for couples and single people who were trying to find their way through the often stormy seas of anxious attachment.

And let's not forget the many researchers, therapists, and scholars who have made this field better through their studies, insights, and caring ways of working with people. They have looked at the links between genes, the environment, trauma, and attachment. This has given them a multidimensional picture of why some of us do this complicated dance of anxious attachment.

---

1. https://www.simplypsychology.org/mary-ainsworth.html

2. https://www.psychologytoday.com/us/therapy-types/emotionally-focused-therap y

In the pages that follow, we'll talk more about these ideas and the experts who helped us understand them. We'll look at how "Childhood Experiences," "The Impact of Trauma," and "The Connection with Personality Disorders" all relate to each other.

• • • ●•● • • •

Childhood Experiences

Imagine wandering through the corridors of a picture museum. Each photo portrays a fleeting moment in a child's life. If you look attentively, you may notice delight, curiosity, dread, or doubt. Those photographs, those frozen moments, form the foundation of who we become. Childhood experiences, in the realm of anxious attachment, are the master strokes that shape the picture.

Childhood experiences are the unseen brush strokes that paint the colors of our attachment patterns. The early connections, exchanges, and relationships set the tone for how we will interact with the world.

Childhood memories take on a vivid and frequently nuanced color in the arena of anxious attachment. Let us dig into these experiences via stories, understanding, and compassion.

• • • ●•● •• •

The Overprotective Nest

Picture yourself as a young person, like four-year-old Alex. Your parents try to keep you safe by making a cocoon around you. Every time you trip or fall, they are quick to help. The world seems dangerous, and their constant watchfulness sends the message that you need to be protected from it. As you get older, the edges of this cocoon start to define your comfort zone. Independence seems like a dream that is hard to reach, and any step beyond its edge makes you nervous. Anxious attachment grows slowly in the nest's safety.

· · · ● · ● · ● · · ·

The Carousel of Inconsistency

Put yourself in Lily's place. Your parents' emotions are all over the place. They can be very close to you one minute and then very far away the next. You become a good observer who can read their moods and guess what they will do next. You learn to walk carefully around possible triggers because the emotional climate is no longer predictable. Your heart beats fast as you try to find your way through this emotional maze and avoid the storm clouds that seem to appear out of nowhere. This constant guessing game makes you feel uneasy, which shows up in your relationships, where you try to find stability in the midst of the chaos. Anxious attachment finds its place in this emotional rollercoaster.

· · · ● · ● · ● · · ·

The Expectations Trap

Imagine growing up as Mark. Your parents have high hopes for how well you do in school, and you work hard to meet their expectations. Trying to be the best becomes a way to win their love and approval. You're afraid of letting them down, and you think your worth depends on how well you do. Even when you're in a relationship, this need to be accepted stays with you. You want reassurance and hope that your partner's affirmation can take away the constant worry that you're not good enough. In the shadow of these hopes and dreams, anxious attachment starts to grow.

· · · ● · ● · ● · · ·

The Dangling Approval

Now, imagine that you are Samantha. Your parents' love and approval feel like rare and valuable gifts that they give you only sometimes. To get these gifts, you have to get good at guessing what they want. The relationship between what you do and how much they like you becomes a delicate dance. Every time someone likes you, it gives you a rush that makes you want more. You constantly worry about losing their love, so you hold on tight to relationships in order to get the reassurance that can make you feel better. In the chase for these gems that hang in the air, anxious attachment grows.

• • • ● • ● • • •

The Echoes of Neglect

Put yourself in Michael's shoes. Your parents are physically present but emotionally distant. Their focus is on something else, which makes you feel like an afterthought. You find comfort in being alone, hiding in books and games. Still, you start to feel empty, which makes you question whether you deserve love. When you're in a relationship, you hold on tight because you're afraid that the emotional distance you felt as a child will happen again. In the echoes of that neglect, anxious attachment grows.

• • • ● • ● • • •

The Struggle of Comparison

Imagine you are Chris. Your parents don't mean to compare you to others, but they do it anyway. The need to be liked turns into a lifelong quest that makes you feel like you're always falling short. You start to believe that you'll never be good enough. In relationships, the fear of not being good enough stays with you, so you try to find validation to stop yourself from comparing yourself to others. As you move through the shadows that these constant measures cast, you start to feel more attached to them.

· · · ● · ● · ● · ·

Seeking Validation

Join Chloe in her world. Your feelings are often ignored, which makes it hard for you to speak up. You start to wonder if your feelings are real because doubt starts to creep in. Your lack of emotional validation affects how you act in relationships. You want reassurance to make up for your past self-doubt. When there isn't any emotional affirmation, anxious attachment gets stronger. This is a response that comes from the echoes of emotional invalidation.

· · · ● · ● · ● · ·

These childhood memories are more than just anecdotes; they are reflections of actual people's lives. They are not deterministic; they are influential. They do not define us, but they do shape us.

Mary Ainsworth's study showed that the intricacies of a caregiver's reaction might be mirrored in a child's behavior. The attentive, the inconsistent, the aloof, the demanding — each leaves a trace, a subtle molding of how a kid views themselves and their position in the world.

Childhood is a time of significant learning and growth. It's a moment when the foundations of connection are being created, brick by brick, experience after experience. Understanding the impact of childhood events on anxious attachment is not about assigning blame or lingering on the past. It's about understanding, compassion, and, eventually, healing.

The painting of our life is never done; it is always being created, moment by moment, decision by choice. Understanding the strokes of our upbringing opens the door to knowing ourselves and the patterns we dance.

So let us keep investigating, hearts open and minds open, as we dig into the next levels of this rich and complicated tapestry.

• • • ● • ● • • •

Impact of Trauma

Trauma. It's a word that sounds like a chilling echo and makes you think of destruction, pain, and a lot of chaos. But what do trauma and anxious attachment have in common? As it turns out, quite a lot.

Think about a clear, peaceful pond. Then someone throws a stone into it, making ripples that break up the calm. This is what trauma does to a person's mind. It's an unexpected stone, an event or series of events that sends shockwaves through the person's emotional world. And these shockwaves can have a big effect on how anxious attachment develops.

Let's walk through the landscapes of trauma and look at how it connects to anxious attachment.

The Unthinkable Betrayals:

Imagine a child who has been physically, emotionally, or sexually abused. People who were meant to protect and care for us are now the ones who hurt us and make us afraid. This betrayal breaks trust and creates a complicated web of anxiety, a desire to connect, and fear of more harm.

The Silent Wounds:

Think about people who have seen violence or lived in a home with a lot of chaos. When you see bad things happen or live in a world where you don't know what will happen next, it can leave you with a feeling of dread. In this situation, anxious attachment becomes a way to find safety, a way to hold on to something in a world that is full of storms.

The Loss That Lasts:

Think about a child who has lost a parent or primary caregiver through death, abandonment, or separation. When someone close to you dies, it can leave a huge hole in your life. This can make you afraid of losing more people and make you watch your relationships closely for signs of abandonment. This fear becomes a key part of a pattern of anxious attachment.

Trauma's Ripple Effect:

Trauma isn't always loud and dramatic; it can also be quiet and sneaky. Chronic neglect, emotional absence, or being constantly told you're not good enough can be quietly damaging. It lowers self-esteem, makes people doubt themselves, and makes them want to be reassured all the time.

Dr. Bessel van der Kolk, a well-known expert on trauma, says that trauma is like "the body keeps the score."[3] It's not just an event that happens and then goes away; it's an experience that stays with you in your mind, body, and soul.

The link between trauma and anxious attachment is not a simple equation. Instead, it is a complicated mix of cause and effect, resilience, and how each person responds. Not everyone who goes through a traumatic event will develop anxious attachment, and not every case of anxious attachment is caused by a traumatic event. But the link between them is real, important, and very human.

Understanding how trauma affects anxious attachment is like turning a kaleidoscope and watching the patterns shift, change, and take on new shapes. It's a view that helps us understand more deeply, act with more compassion, and connect with more empathy.

Let's walk carefully, keep our hearts open, and have a lot of respect for the strength of the human spirit as we explore this sensitive area. On the way from trauma to healing, there are many obstacles, but there are also lots of chances to learn, grow, and change.

---

3. van der Kolk, Bessel (2015). The Body Keeps the Score: Brain, Mind, and Body in the Healing of Trauma. Penguin Books.

· · · ● · ● · ● · ·

Connection with Personality Disorders

In a garden full of colorful flowers, each bloom shows a different person. Some are big and bold, some are soft and sweet, and some have thorns hiding in them. The garden of a person's personality is a complex ecosystem where their actions, thoughts, and feelings all mix together to make the many ways they show who they are.

But what happens when certain patterns become fixed, hard to break and cause pain or trouble? We move into the complicated and often misunderstood world of personality disorders.

Let's now consider anxious attachment. It can connect and affect many different parts of personality disorders, like a vine with many branches. Let's learn more about this complicated link by weaving in real-life stories and expert opinions.

Borderline Personality Disorder (BPD):

Imagine a person standing on the edge of a cliff, feeling both the pull of the abyss and the longing for solid ground. Someone with BPD lives in a world like that. This disorder is characterized by emotional instability, a strong fear of abandonment, and a pattern of unstable relationships. Dr. Marsha Linehan, who came up with Dialectical Behavior Therapy (DBT)[4], has looked into how BPD and anxious attachment are related. When the constant need for closeness is mixed with the fear of being rejected or left alone, it can cause a whirlwind of feelings that are similar to the way anxious attachment works.

Avoidant Personality Disorder:

Imagine someone stuck in a shell, wanting to connect but paralyzed by fear and inadequacy. This is what avoidant personality disorder is. Even though it seems

---

4. Linehan, Marsha M. (2014). DBT Skills Training Manual. The Guilford Press

counterintuitive, anxious attachment can also be a factor here. People can avoid people because they are afraid of being criticized or rejected, but they still want to connect, which creates an inner tug-of-war.

Obsessive-Compulsive Personality Disorder (OCPD):

Imagine a world where control, perfection, and order are the most important things. That's what OCPD looks like. Anxious attachment could show up here as a strong fear of losing control and a stubbornness that comes from deep-seated anxiety. Schema Therapy by Dr. Jeffrey Young[5] has shown how problems with early attachment can lead to rigid and perfectionist patterns like those seen in OCPD.

Narcissistic Personality Disorder:

Imagine a mirror that only shows you what you want to see and hides your fears and weaknesses. That's how people with Narcissistic Personality Disorder see the world. Under the arrogance and focus on self, there may be a fragile sense of self-worth that is easily hurt by criticism and rejection. These shadows can hide anxious attachment, which makes people want to be liked and validated.

These links between anxious attachment and personality disorders are like intricate threads in a big tapestry. They don't define or explain everything, but they give a nuanced look at how personality, attachment, and mental health work together in a complicated way.

Let's keep looking into this with an open mind and a kind heart, knowing that the garden of a person's personality is full of both challenges and beauty, pain and growth. The stories we find and the connections we make are all part of what it means to be a person.

Are we ready to delve deeper into the world of anxious attachment, knowing that every layer we peel back reveals more about ourselves and each other? The journey continues.

---

5. https://www.psychologytoday.com/us/therapy-types/schema-therapy#:~:text= Schema%20therapy%20is%20a%20type, struggle%20to%20maintain%20adult%20relationships.

CHAPTER TWO

TYPES AND STAGES OF ANXIOUS ATTACHMENT

Understanding Different Types of Anxious Attachment

Anxious attachment is more than just a term used in psychology; it is a real thing that many people go through. To learn about the different kinds of anxious attachment, we need to look at both well-known theories and new ideas in the field.

Attachment Theory Foundation

When talking about anxious attachment, you can't leave out the work of British psychiatrist John Bowlby, who laid the groundwork for attachment theory. Bowlby's work emphasized how important the relationship between a child and their caretaker is and how problems in these early relationships can lead to anxious patterns in later relationships.

Take Sarah, a young woman in her late 20s, as an example. Sarah's parents were loving, but they never knew what would happen. Sometimes they were caring and close, and sometimes they were far away and hard to reach. This lack of consistency made Sarah worry that she would be left alone. Now that she's an adult, she needs constant reassurance from her partners, which is a sign of an anxious attachment.

The Role of Trauma

Anxious attachment isn't just caused by problems in childhood. This attachment style can also be caused by trauma, whether it happened when the person was a child or as an adult.

Take the story of James, a war veteran who saw how horrible war can be. When he got back home, he found that his relationships were affected by a new kind of worry. He was afraid that anyone he loves could be taken away at any time because he had lost close friends on the battlefield. Because of his anxious attachment, he had to check on his family members all the time and couldn't relax until he knew they were safe.

Emerging Perspectives and Complexity

Understanding of anxious attachment keeps getting better, and new studies show how complicated it is. Some psychologists say that anxious attachment isn't just one type, but that it can be broken down into subtypes that have different causes and ways of acting.

Think about what Dr. Karen, a therapist who specializes in attachment issues, has to say. She has seen that her clients' anxious attachment isn't always caused by fear of being left alone. For some, it's about feeling good about themselves and being seen as valuable. For others, it's about being very aware of their partner's mood and needs. The anxiety is the same at its core, but it shows up in different ways.

By looking at the different parts of anxious attachment, we can start to see that it's not a simple idea. It has many different parts and is affected by things like upbringing, trauma, and even genes.

The Influence of Genetics and Environmental Factors

Nature vs. nurture has always been at the heart of trying to figure out how people act, and anxious attachment is no different. Even though we know a lot about the different types of anxious attachment from theories and our own experiences, genetics and the environment add more layers to this complicated phenomenon.

Genetic Influence

Anxious attachment is often caused by genes that aren't fully understood. It's not a specific gene that causes anxiety. Instead, it's a tendency that can make a person more likely to have this attachment style.

Take the case of Laura and Maria, who are twins. Laura's attachment style is anxious, while Maria's is not. This is because Laura grew up in the same loving family with consistent care, while Maria did not. When we looked more closely, we saw that Laura's anxious habits were shared by other family members from different generations. Even though Laura's anxious attachment wasn't caused by her genes alone, they probably made her more likely to have it.

Environmental Triggers

Even though genes can set the stage for anxious attachment, environmental factors often act as triggers. These things can be anything from cultural pressures to certain events in a person's life.

Alex is a young man who grew up in a culture that put a lot of value on strong family ties and tight-knit communities. Even though this environment encouraged love and connection, it also made people feel like they had to fit in with what society expected of them. Alex was afraid of not meeting these expectations, which made him anxious in his relationships. He was always trying to please others over his own needs.

How genes and the environment work together

The interaction between genes and the environment is one of the most complicated parts of anxious attachment. It's not a simple equation, but a dynamic relationship between two things that can make each other stronger.

Take the case of Lily, a young woman who comes from a family where anxiety disorders are common. As a child, Lily was bullied at school. This was a stressful event that triggered her genetic tendency toward anxiety. She ended up with an anxious attachment style, where she was always worried about whether her friends would stay loyal and accept her.

A Complicated Dance

Anxious attachment is not formed in a straight line. It's a dance between genetic traits and environmental factors, with each person's own experiences setting the steps. When we realize that there's no one-size-fits-all explanation for anxious attachment, we can look at it from a more nuanced point of view.

· · · ● · ● · · ·

A Journey Through Life: The Stages of Anxious Attachment

Anxious attachment doesn't stay the same; it changes and adapts as you go through different stages of life. Understanding this progression helps us not only find people with anxious attachment, but also give them the right kind of help at the right time in their lives.

Childhood: The Foundation of Attachment

Attachment patterns, including anxious attachment, are often thought to have their roots in childhood. The way a child interacts with their primary caregivers sets the stage for how they will interact with other people in the future.

Emily is a young child whose parents work a lot. Emily's time at daycare is stressful because she doesn't know when her parents will pick her up. Because of this early experience, she grows up to fear being left alone and becomes too attached to the people she loves.

Adolescence: Navigating Social Complexity

The teenage years are hard because people want to be independent and try to fit in with their friends. During this stage, anxious attachment can become clear.

Jake is a high school student who has always been a little shy. As Jake's friendships get more complicated and he starts to like girls, his underlying worry about being attached comes to the surface. He obsesses over what his friends think of him and is always looking for confirmation and reassurance.

Adulthood: Relationships, Work, and Self-Identity

Anxious attachment often gets worse as people get older, especially in romantic relationships, friendships, and even the workplace.

Take Sarah, who has a successful job but can't stop thinking about emails and texts from her partner. Her anxiety follows her to work, where she is always trying to get approval from her boss and coworkers. Both her personal and professional relationships are based on a theme of anxious attachment.

Later Life: Reflection and Transformation

Anxious attachment doesn't always go away as people get older; instead, it may change. The challenges and knowledge that come with getting older can change how anxious attachment is shown.

George is a retired man who has always had trouble with his relationships. The passage of time and the loss of a loved one have given me a new point of view. George now uses his anxious energy to connect with his grandchildren and his community in a positive way. He has turned his once-disabling attachment style into a way to connect with others and show compassion.

A Lifelong Companion

Anxious attachment is not just a passing feeling or a phase. It goes with you through life, affecting and being affected by different stages. Recognizing this fluidity makes it possible to help people with anxious attachment in a more empathetic and effective way, recognizing that it's not a problem to be fixed but a part of human complexity that needs to be understood and cared for.

CHAPTER THREE

THE INFLUENCE OF GENDER ROLES, SOCIAL MEDIA, AND MODERN CULTURE

Gender Roles and Anxious Attachment - A Spectrum of Influence

Gender roles, which are societal norms about what behaviors, attitudes, and activities are acceptable for each gender, have a big effect on how people feel and show anxious attachment. All genders are affected by this, which shows how cultural expectations and personal identity interact in a complicated way.

Traditional Gender Roles:

Men and Masculinity:

Traditional ideas of what it means to be a man tend to focus on stoicism, strength, and holding back emotions. This can make things hard for men who have trouble forming close relationships.

For example, James is a man who has trouble with anxious attachment but feels pressure from society to seem strong and unaffected. He always wants his partner to reassure him, but he is too embarrassed to talk about his fears. He is stuck between his true feelings and what society expects of him.

Women and Femininity:

Traditional femininity, on the other hand, often focuses on caring for others, being emotionally open, and making connections.

Take Lisa, who thinks that society expects her to be the emotional center of her relationships. Her anxious attachment shows up as a focus on pleasing others and caring for others to the point of not caring for herself. This is because of a cultural story that says women are valued for their caring roles.

Non-Binary and Non-Conforming Gender Perspectives

The spectrum of gender is very wide, and traditional binary roles don't cover the wide range of experiences of people who don't fit into either of the two categories.

Taylor is a genderqueer person whose fearful attachment is made worse by the fact that society has a hard time fitting them into traditional gender roles. Their relationship anxiety is often tied to how they see themselves and how others see and treat them. Taylor's story is a powerful example of how gender norms can make anxious attachment even harder to deal with.

The Changing Scenery of Gender

In today's world, our ideas about gender are changing. They are becoming more open and less tied to strict roles and stereotypes. This change gives new ways of thinking about anxious attachment, taking into account the different challenges and opportunities that men and women may face.

Alex, a transgender man, deals with his anxious attachment by looking at it through the lens of his transition. His experience is shaped not only by how he relates to other people but also by how society as a whole views gender differences.

An Interwoven Web of Influences

There are many different ways that gender affects anxious attachment. The relationship between gender and anxious attachment is complicated and multifaceted, from the traditional roles that shape men's and women's lives to the unique perspectives of non-binary and gender-diverse people.

· · · ● · ● · · ·

Social Media and Digital Connections - A Double-Edged Sword

In the digitally connected world we live in now, social media platforms and instant messaging are important parts of how we interact with each other. This change has had big effects on anxious attachment. Depending on how they are used, they can act as a magnifying glass or a soothing balm.

The Amplification of Anxiety

Constant Connectivity:

Because social media lets us stay in touch all the time, it has given rise to new worries. Imagine Stephanie, who finds herself obsessively checking her partner's last seen status on a messaging app. Every minute that goes by without a reply makes her worry about him grow, and a simple delay turns into a whirlwind of doubts and fears.

Comparison and Perfectionism:

Social media sites like Instagram and Facebook often show idealized versions of relationships and ways of life. When David, a young man with anxious attachment, compares his relationships to the picture-perfect ones he sees online, he starts to doubt himself. The difference between what you see on your screen and what you see in real life can make you feel anxious and set unrealistic standards and expectations.

As the popular Internet meme says: "Stop Comparing Your Behind-The-Scenes With Everyone's Highlight Reel"

The Potential for Healing

Online Communities and Support:

On the other hand, the digital world also gives people new ways to connect and help each other. Lily has had trouble with anxious attachment for years, but an online support group helps her feel better. This online community gives people a place to understand, feel empathy for, and talk about their own experiences. This makes the digital world a healing place.

Therapeutic Tools and Apps:

Technology isn't just a way to connect with people; it's also a way to grow and heal on a personal level. Mark has been struggling with anxious attachment for a long time. He finds an app that helps people become more self-aware and mindful. This digital tool helps him on his way to getting better, which shows how technology can be used to help people grow in a good way.

How to Find Your Way in the Digital Landscape

Social media, digital connections, and anxious attachment don't have a completely good or bad relationship with each other. It's a complicated landscape that shows how complicated human relationships are in the digital age.

The digital world has both challenges and opportunities. Constant connectivity and idealized portrayals can make worries worse, while online communities and therapeutic tools can help people heal and grow.

Modern Culture and Changing Dynamics: Finding Your Way in a Changing World

Modern culture is characterized by fast change, individualism, and changing rules about how to connect with other people. These changes in culture present both problems and chances for people with anxious attachment.

The Culture of Individualism

In a society that values independence and success more and more, anxious attachment can become more noticeable.

Think about Maria, a young professional who grew up in a society that values independence and personal success. Her anxious attachment often goes against what society tells her, which is that she should be self-sufficient. This causes her inner conflict and anxiety in her relationships. The struggle between needing other people and wanting to be on your own shows a larger cultural problem.

The Hookup Culture and Casual Relationships

The rise of hookup culture and casual relationships has made it harder for people who have trouble with attachment anxiety to find their way.

This is shown by Tom's story. He gets stuck in a cycle of short-term relationships because of a cultural trend that often values casual connections over deep emotional bonds. Modern dating is always setting off his anxious attachment, which is made worse by his deep-seated need for stability and connection.

How Work-Life Balance and Modern Lifestyles Affect Us

Modern ways of life, with their busy schedules and focus on work, can make anxious attachment worse.

Rebecca is a hard-working woman who is married, but she struggles with anxious attachment. Her relationship is strained by the demands of her job and the idea that she should be able to "have it all." This adds to her underlying worries. Her story shows how hard it is to stay emotionally healthy in a culture that often puts work ahead of personal life.

Adapting and being aware in a world that is changing

With its changing norms and values, modern culture makes it hard for people to deal with anxious attachment. From the focus on individualism to the rise of short-term relationships to the demands of modern lifestyles, the world we live in today presents both unique challenges and chances to grow.

CHAPTER FOUR

COPING WITH COMMON PROBLEMS: CLINGINESS, JEALOUSY, AND FEAR OF ABANDONMENT

Understanding the Common Problems

Identifying the Symptoms

Anxious attachment shows up in a number of different ways that can be both bothersome and upsetting. Here are some important signs:

Clinginess:

In the context of anxious attachment, being clingy isn't just about being too affectionate; it's also about having a strong fear of losing connection. This can show up in things like constantly checking for messages, needing to be reassured, and finding it hard to be apart from a partner. It can have a big effect on both people in the relationship, leading to stress and dissatisfaction.

Realizing that someone is too attached is just the first step. We'll talk more about how different ways of dealing with this problem can help us turn a potential weakness into a way to grow.

Jealousy:

In the context of anxious attachment, jealousy is more than just a little bit of envy; it's a constant fear that can take over a relationship. This could mean having unfounded fears and a constant need to be reassured.

How do we deal with this complicated feeling? Later in this book, we'll talk about effective ways to build trust and confidence, using the pain of jealousy to make things better.

Fear of Abandonment:

The fear of being abandoned isn't just a worry; it's a terrifying terror that can lead to actions that, ironically, push people away. This fear can ruin relationships and leave scars that are hard to get rid of even after they end.

How can we get over such a strong fear? Keep reading, because we'll talk about tools and ideas that can help you not only deal with this fear but also turn it into a way to grow personally and improve your relationships.

· · · ● · ● · · ·

Clinginess: A Day in the Life of Richard

Setting:

A bustling city, filled with coffee shops, parks, and office buildings. Richard, a charismatic yet anxiously attached man, navigates his day with one goal in mind: getting attention from his love interest, Sam.

Act 1: The Morning Text Crisis

Richard's thoughts: "Should I text Sam 'Good morning' with one smiley face or three? Oh no, maybe three is too much? What if two is not enough? Two and a half? How does one even make a half-smiley face?"

Act 2: The Coffee Shop Conundrum

Richard's thoughts: "If I just 'accidentally' bump into Sam at her favorite coffee shop and casually bring up that documentary we both like, will it seem too planned? What if I wear my 'I love documentaries' shirt? Too obvious?"

Act 3: Social Media Stalking... Err, Research

Richard's thoughts: "If I like Sam's post from 47 weeks ago, will it seem creepy? What if I like the one from 49 weeks instead? Oh wait, what's this? A picture of a dog? Sam loves dogs! I should get a dog. No, two dogs. No, a cat and a dog!"

Act 4: The Office Water Cooler Catastrophe

Richard's thoughts: "If I time my water cooler visit to coincide with Sam's, I can ask about her weekend. But what if I spill the water? Or what if the cooler is empty? Should I bring my own water? What if I bring sparkling water and offer Sam a glass? No, that's too James Bond-ish. Or is it?"

Act 5: The Gym Dilemma

Richard's thoughts: "If I just happen to be at the gym when Sam is, I can show off my 'casual' workout routine. But should I do cardio or weights? Both? At the same time? Can one run on the treadmill while lifting dumbbells? Is that a thing?"

Conclusion: The Day's End

As the sun sets, Richard's day of overthinking, overplanning, and overdoing comes to an end. The mission to get Sam's attention was filled with comedic missteps and quirky dilemmas. The lesson? Anxious attachment might not lead to smooth sailing, but it sure makes for a hilarious adventure!

Analyzing Richard's Adventure:

Richard's day was full of funny things, but it was also an emotional roller coaster that wore him out. His worries made every choice, no matter how small, worse. Let's break down what was going on and think about how to deal with these worries.

Overthinking Every Interaction

What Happened:

Richard worried about texts, conversations in coffee shops, and even things that happened at the water cooler. His mind was racing with possibilities, turning simple decisions into complex dilemmas.

Coping Strategies:

To stop himself from overthinking, Richard could use techniques that help him stay in the present. By focusing on the here and now, he can learn to respond naturally instead of getting lost in endless "what-ifs."

Focusing too much on details

What Happened:

Richard's obsession with small details, like the number of smiley faces in a text or the right time to go to the water cooler, made even simple decisions feel hard.

Coping Strategies:

Focusing on self-compassion and acceptance can help him see that he doesn't have to be perfect. Mistakes and weird habits are part of being human, and if you accept them, your interactions will be more genuine and less stressful.

Trying Too Hard to Impress

What Happened:

Whether at the gym or the coffee shop, Richard's desire to impress Sam led to ideas that were funny but not very useful.

Coping Strategies:

Richard can feel better about himself if he focuses on being real and having respect for himself. He won't feel the need to put on a show if he values himself and his interests.

Misinterpreting Normal Social Cues

What Happened:

Normal social cues became confusing and hard for Richard to figure out what they meant. He made complicated plans because he thought too much about simple things.

Coping Strategies:

Richard can avoid misunderstandings by getting better at talking to people and asking for more information when he isn't sure. Open dialogue helps people get to know each other without having to play guessing games.

How to Get to Simple and Real

Richard's day was funny, but it wore him out. It showed how complicated anxious attachment is and how it can make even simple decisions seem like hard things to do. But people with anxious attachment can get through their relationships with more ease and joy if they use coping skills like mindfulness, self-compassion, authenticity, and clear communication.

· · · · ● · ● · · ·

Jealousy: The Green-Eyed Monster

Jealousy is a complicated feeling with many different facets. Even though it's a normal response when we feel threatened or unsafe, it turns into a "green-eyed monster" when it controls our thoughts and actions. In the world of anxious attachment, jealousy can be particularly strong because of fears of being abandoned and an insatiable need for validation. Imagine a young woman who is always checking her boyfriend's phone, not because she is interested, but because she is terrified that he will leave her. Her jealousy is more than just a feeling; it haunts her every day.

What makes people jealous?

The Roots:

In anxious attachment, jealousy doesn't just pop up out of nowhere. Imagine a young child being left by a parent. That deep wound can fester as the child grows up, leading to jealousy. The need to control, the terror of losing loved ones, all stem from that early trauma.

Manifestations:

Jealousy can show up in small ways, like a creased brow when a partner talks to someone else, or in big ways, like an explosive argument. It's like a creature that can change its form but is always there.

Relationships and Jealousy

Romantic Relationships:

A man finds himself losing sleep over his partner's new coworker. Every laugh they share and every look they give each other hurts him deeply. His jealousy isn't just about his partner; it's also about how he feels about himself and what he's afraid of.

Family and Friendships:

Jealousy can ruin even the best friendships. When self-esteem is low, a friend's success or a sibling's achievement can make someone feel jealous.

Coping Strategies

Self-awareness:

It takes courage to deal with jealousy. It means looking at yourself in the mirror and seeing your scars, fears, and feelings of insecurity. Writing in a journal, meditating, or just taking a moment to think can change your life.

Communication:

If you're feeling jealous, talk to your partner about it in a loving way. It's more important to say "I'm scared and I need you" than "You're wrong and I'm mad."

Building trust:

It takes time to build trust. It's a garden that has been cared for over time. It has been watered with honesty, given light with vulnerability, and grown in soil full of empathy.

Jealousy in Open and Polyamorous Relationships

A Different Setting:

Jealousy isn't just about one partner in a polyamorous relationship; it's a web. It means learning how to keep your feelings, needs, and boundaries in check across many connections.

Communication is Important:

Imagine a family meeting where everyone sits down and talks about how they feel, what worries them, and what makes them happy. Jealousy doesn't bother you because you are so honest.

Embracing Compersion:

Compersion is often referred to as the opposite of jealousy. It's the feeling of joy one experiences when witnessing or knowing about a loved one's joy, happiness, or pleasure with another person. In a romantic context, this can mean feeling genuine happiness for a partner's excitement, pleasure, or emotional connection with another partner, rather than feeling jealous or threatened.

Compersion can be a very valuable and enriching emotional experience for people in polyamorous or open relationships, where they may have more than one romantic or sexual partner. It's a change from seeing love and affection as a limited resource that could lead to competition between partners to seeing love as big and full of different things.

An Example of Compersion

Imagine a woman in a polyamorous relationship who knows her partner is going out with someone else he is seeing. She doesn't feel jealous or insecure about him. Instead, she feels happy and excited for him. She's really glad that he's exploring this relationship and finding happiness in it. This is what compersion is.

Compersion and Anxious Attachment

People with anxious attachment may find it harder to feel compersion because of their fears and insecurities. But it's not impossible either. Even if it feels strange at first, people can learn to develop compersion with effort, communication, building trust, and sometimes professional help.

Growth and Help for the Individual:

Open and multi-partner relationships require growth. To find your way along this unique path, you need to think about yourself, get help from your community, and sometimes get professional advice.

Getting the Green-Eyed Monster Under Control

Getting rid of jealousy is a process, not a goal. It's a process of growth, empathy, building trust, and self-compassion that never ends. In both monogamous and non-monogamous relationships, self-awareness, love, and connection are the keys to moving forward.

• • • ● • ● • • • ·

Fear of Abandonment: A Phantom in the Shadows

A Fear with Deep Roots

People who are afraid of being abandoned don't just feel anxious; they also feel a deep ache in their hearts. It's like a ghost that hangs around relationships and whispers insecurities into the ears of people who don't want to be abandoned.

Meet Tom. Sarah, Tom's partner, comes home late one night. He is not angry; he's terrified. The fear isn't about betrayal; it's about losing the one person who makes him feel whole. Each minute feels like an hour, and his mind races with worst-case scenarios. This is the reality of living with the fear of abandonment.

Where the fear came from

Tom's fear didn't start with Sarah. It began in his childhood when his father left the family. That early rejection planted a seed of doubt that grew into a towering tree of fear. Later, a painful breakup with a high school sweetheart watered that tree, embedding the fear deeper.

How it affects relationships

Tom's fear gets in the way of his relationship with Sarah, making it harder for them to be together. He always needs to be reassured, emotionally clings to her and is very sensitive to any sign of distance. It's not because he's controlling; he's afraid, and that fear drives him.

Fear is there even between friends. He once sent a friend a birthday gift and then worried for days, not about whether the friend liked it, but whether the gift was enough to cement their friendship.

Coping Strategies

For Tom and many other people like him, the first step is to be aware. He has to accept that the fear is there and figure out where it comes from. He needs to know why he's scared. It's not enough to know that he's scared.

Building trust with Sarah is crucial. They work on communicating, being honest, and committing to each other. They make rules, and they stick to them. The foundation of their relationship gets stronger over time.

But sometimes he needs help from a professional. Tom's therapist helps him figure out what's behind his fear by looking at his childhood, his past relationships, and how he acts now. The process isn't easy or quick, but it changes things.

From Being Afraid to Being Free

Tom's journey from fear to freedom is not a straight line. It's a long, winding road with both ups and downs. He never gets over his fear of being abandoned, but he learns to live with it, deal with it, and grow from it. He doesn't feel safe by clinging to other people, but by getting to know himself and making strong, healthy connections.

Hope and healing are not just possible, they are also within reach. The fear of being abandoned can be faced, understood, and tamed through self-awareness, hard work in relationships, and sometimes professional help.

CHAPTER FIVE

PART II: NAVIGATING RELATIONSHIPS WITH ANXIOUS ATTACHMENT

DATING AND INTIMACY

How Anxious Attachment Changes the Dating Scene

Dating, the exciting ups and downs of feelings, making dinner decisions, and wondering if spinach is stuck between your teeth. But for people with anxious attachment, dating isn't just a ride; it's a maze full of self-doubt, anticipation, and a dozen "what ifs."

Problems in a Relationship:

The world of dating has never been easy, but when you have anxious attachment, you have to worry not only about what to wear but also about whether your date will call you back and whether you're coming on too strong or not strong enough. The challenge is to find a balance between being too clingy because of anxiety and having a real connection.

When we face our fears head-on, we experience an interesting contrast. Growing up, I was always torn between wanting to have a girlfriend and doing everything I could to keep me from getting one.

You see, for me, asking a girl out was never just a simple question; it was always a test of who I was. Every look, smile, and rejection showed who I was or, more accurately, who I thought I was. The fear of being rejected was more than just fear; it showed how insecure I was.

I can still remember the first time I was brave enough to ask a girl out. My heart was a chaotic symphony, a pounding drum that seemed determined to get out of my chest. My hands were wet, and I could barely whisper. In those few seconds, I felt like a lifetime of doubt was on my shoulders.

When she finally said she would go out with me, I felt like I had won the lottery. But here's the paradox: I kept hearing this voice in the back of my head telling me it was too good to be true. Thoughts of worry went around and around like a tornado, making a storm of worries.

I did everything I could to stop the relationship from happening before it even started. Did I call too much? Was I in a hurry? Were you happy? I looked at everything she said, did, and said, looking for signs that she wasn't interested anymore.

My actions caused them to come true. I didn't want to lose her, so I moved away from her. My constant need for reassurance, my constant need to check for messages, and my irrational jealousy all pushed us apart. Our relationship lasted all of 9 days and I was heartbroken when she ended it (not that I blame her one bit).

When I look back, I can see that my anxious attachment wasn't just based on fear; it was a weird dance between wanting something and being afraid of losing it. I really wanted to connect, but I was afraid of it. I wanted closeness, but I didn't think I deserved it.

I had to think about myself, grow, and learn for years before I could see the patterns that had held me captive. I learned to see my value, trust in love, and enjoy the beauty of being vulnerable without letting fear tell me how to dance.

My path wasn't easy, but it was very worthwhile. It helped me go from feeling anxious to feeling like I had a real connection with someone. It taught me that love isn't just about finding the right person; it's also about becoming the right person.

My story is just one thread in the big picture of life. But it's a theme that many people who have trouble with anxious attachment can relate to. It shows how strong the human spirit is, how resilient we all are, and how important it is to find out who you are.

In the mid-2020s, with all of the swipes and choices that come with online dating, things only get more complicated. Every message that isn't answered can feel like a rejection, and every late response can feel like a judgment. The screen can act as a barrier, blocking empathy and making the distance between people even bigger.

The Initial Stages of Love:

Getting to know someone, in the beginning, is like walking a tightrope. On the one hand, people want to open up, let their guard down, and connect. On the other hand, there's the fear of rejection, the nagging worry that you'll be too much or not enough.

For people who have trouble forming attachments, these early stages can be especially scary. The desire to connect fights with the fear of being left alone, making a dance that is both beautiful and scary. It's like dancing a waltz on a tightrope. You have to be self-aware, trust others, and be brave.

When Mark met Sarah, they hit it off right away. But his anxious attachment meant that every unreturned text was a potential sign of disinterest, every canceled plan a rejection. The thrill of a new love came with a bit of fear, and each step forward was clouded by doubt.

But dating with anxious attachment is not just a challenge; it's an opportunity. It gives you a chance to learn about yourself, face your fears, and grow. Mark, Sarah, myself, and many others use dating as a way to learn about ourselves and find out what love is, how trust is built, and what genuine connection feels like.

When you date with anxious attachment, there are ups and downs, successes and failures. But it's a terrain that can be mastered with self-awareness, empathy, and a willingness to embrace both the joy and the uncertainty of love's first steps.

Sexuality & Intimacy Dynamics

Intimacy is a dance. Trust, openness, and connection are gracefully intertwined. But when anxiety enters the room, the dance can turn into a wrestling match. Let's look at how anxious attachment can affect this delicate balance in relationships and how it played out in my own life.

Fear of Vulnerability

Intimacy can be both good and bad for someone with anxious attachment. On the one hand, it's the answer to a deep desire for connection. On the other hand, it exposes the self in a terrible way.

When I was younger, getting close to someone was a battleground. I wanted to be close, but the closer we got, the more I felt exposed. Every touch, every shared secret, and every loving glance could be a minefield. I was afraid that if I let someone in, they would see my flaws and run.

The Need for Reassurance

People who are anxiously attached often need constant reassurance that they are loved, wanted, and valued. This need can show up in different ways, like constantly wanting compliments or always wanting to be touched.

I remember a relationship where my need for reassurance was all-consuming. I would constantly seek confirmation and fish for compliments, needing to know that I was loved and wanted. I needed to hear it again and over again; it wasn't enough to just feel it. It turned into a cycle, a never-ending hunger.

Intimacy in the Bedroom

For someone with anxious attachment, sexuality in particular can become a complicated dance. The need for physical connection is strong, but so is the fear of being rejected or abandoned.

In my experience, sex was frequently a source of both joy and distress. The physical connection was exciting, but I was always waiting for the other shoe to drop. Was I up to the task? Did she enjoy it? Was this the start of the end? These questions would keep me up at night, turning what should have been a loving experience into a source of stress.

Moving Toward Healthy Intimacy

Even with anxious attachment, it is possible to cultivate healthy intimacy despite the difficulties. It requires self-compassion, communication, trust, and awareness.

For me, the path to healthy intimacy was a path of healing. It was about learning to trust myself as well as others. It was about realizing that being open to being hurt is not a sign of weakness but a strength. It was about realizing that love is a gift, not a test.

Handling Breakups and Moving from Toxic to Healthy Relationships

Breakups are never easy, but they can be a whirlwind of confusion, despair, and self-doubt for someone with anxious attachment. When the fear of being abandoned comes true, the emotional fallout can be very strong. Here is how my life's journey went and what I learned along the way.

The Pain of Being Shunned

When a relationship ends, it's normal to feel like you've lost something. For me, that loss was made worse by a crippling fear that I was unlovable. Every breakup was not just the end of something; it was also a judgment and a confirmation of my deepest fears.

I remember a particularly painful breakup in which I felt not only rejected but also discarded. It felt as though all my hard work, love, and willingness to be vulnerable had been for nothing. I fell into a pit of self-doubt and started to question everything about myself.

The Dangers of Toxic Relationships

Fear of being abandoned and the need to feel important can sometimes lead to a pattern of toxic relationships. I was drawn to unhealthy relationships where I was mistreated or undervalued. I ignored warning signs, disregarded my gut, and settled for less than I deserved because I so desperately wanted to be loved.

The Path to Recovery

It's not easy to switch from toxic to healthy relationships. It's a journey of self-discovery, self-respect, and self-love. It took me years to recognize the patterns that were holding me back, to realize that I deserved love, and to learn how to set boundaries.

I had to learn to tell the difference between love and obsession, between caring and control. I had to learn how to tell if a relationship was healthy and how to trust myself enough to leave those that weren't.

Embracing Positive Relationships

With a better understanding of what love is, what it takes, and what it gives, I now stand on the other side of that journey. I've learned to value genuine connection, respect, and emotional maturity.

I've learned that healthy relationships aren't about holding on or being in charge, but rather about helping each other and growing. They're about accepting the beautiful flaws in ourselves and in each other and creating a strong, loving, and true bond.

Strategies for Self-Improvement

Anxious attachment can make dating a maze of traps and dead ends. But I've learned over the years that with the right attitude and tools, it's possible to create a path to healthier relationships.

Building Self-Esteem:

It was important to know what I was worth and what I could bring to a relationship. I learned to see myself as a whole person worthy of love by focusing on my strengths and accepting my flaws.

Improving Communication:

Communication must be open, honest, and respectful. I was able to connect with people more deeply by learning to express my feelings without fear or reluctance.

Setting Boundaries:

Knowing my limits and being able to say them clearly was a crucial first step. Boundaries are not walls; they are rules that encourage respect and understanding between people.

Perspectives from Partners

When I thought back on past relationships, I realized that anxious attachment affects not only me but also my partners. I got in touch with a few of them, and their perspectives were eye-opening.

One former partner said, "It was like riding a roller coaster to date you. Although the love was strong, there were times when the worries were too much to handle. I was able to see the person behind your fear by understanding your anxious attachment."

Professional Advice

One doesn't have to figure out how to deal with the complexities of anxious attachment on their own when dating. Many mental health professionals and relationship counselors are skilled at helping people with anxious attachment patterns. Self-awareness, vulnerability, and empathy are frequently emphasized.

Therapists often advise patients to talk openly with their partners about their fears and insecurities. Techniques like cognitive-behavioral therapy (CBT) and mindfulness can also help foster healthier, more satisfying relationships.

Those who struggle with anxious attachment can learn tools and strategies that help them connect with others in more balanced and meaningful ways by getting professional help.

Hope and development are emphasized.

The path to healthier relationships has been long and winding, but it has been worth every step. My approach to love has changed as a result of self-reflection, professional advice, and a strong belief in myself.

I want readers to know that anxious attachment is not a sentence for life; rather, it's an opportunity for growth, understanding, and deep connection. There is hope, joy, and love out there, and we all have what it takes to find it.

CHAPTER SIX

COGNITIVE BEHAVIORAL THERAPY AND DATING FOR THE ANXIOUSLY ATTACHED

CBT in Relationships: An Introduction

For those struggling with anxious attachment, dating can be incredibly scary. It can be difficult to deal with the nerves, "what-ifs," and second thoughts. But what if there were a map or guide to help you find your way through the turns and twists of love? Cognitive-Behavioral Therapy (CBT) is a well-known type of therapy that focuses on how people think and behave. It could be the tool that many people need.

Cognitive-Behavioral Therapy (CBT) Unveiled

CBT is a practical, evidence-based approach to understanding and changing thought and behavior patterns. At its core, CBT is about recognizing unhelpful thoughts and learning how to challenge and replace them with more realistic and positive ones.

Relationships and Anxious Attachment: Relevance

When it comes to dating, people with anxious attachment are frequently caught in a web of limiting beliefs and actions that hurt them. The fear of rejection, the propensity to overthink every interaction, and the constant worry about what the other person is thinking all contribute to a stressful dating experience. CBT helps untangle this web of thoughts by giving people a way to recognize and change how they think about them.

Imagine, for example, that you are waiting for a text from someone you are interested in. As the hours pass, the mind begins to spin: "They don't like me. I made a mistake. It's over." But CBT teaches us to stop and question these thoughts, which allows for a more balanced view: "Maybe they're busy. Maybe they didn't see my message. I don't know enough to make a decision."

Tools and Techniques to Come: Setting the Scene

In this chapter, we'll look at how CBT principles can be used to address the particular difficulties of dating with anxious attachment. We're about to start a journey toward more mindful and empowered connections, from understanding limiting beliefs to doing practical exercises for growth.

Fundamentals of CBT for Dating

Modern dating can be full of both heartbreaking lows and exhilarating highs. The lows can feel especially overwhelming for those with anxious attachment. Understanding how Cognitive-Behavioral Therapy (CBT) can be used to address the particular difficulties of dating can be helpful.

Thoughts, feelings, and actions make up the cognitive triad.

The Cognitive Triad, which explains how thoughts, feelings, and actions are all connected, is the foundation of cognitive behavioral therapy. Here's how it works in dating:

- **Thoughts:** "She hasn't responded; she must not like me."

- **Emotions:** Feeling rejected, anxious, or sad.

- **Behaviors:** Checking the phone obsessively, or maybe withdrawing from dating altogether.

A healthier dating life requires identifying and addressing these connections.

The Influence of Automatic Thoughts

Automatic thoughts are the quick, unthought-out beliefs that come to our minds. They may appear in dating as "I'm unlovable", "They forgot about me", or "They're out of my league." The problem is that these thoughts can lead to self-sabotage. CBT gives you tools to challenge and reframe these automatic thoughts, which makes it easier to connect in a more real and powerful way.

Core Beliefs and Their Role in Relationships

The fundamental ideas that shape how we see ourselves and the world are known as core beliefs. Perhaps you've always thought that you have to prove yourself in relationships or that love means pain. These core beliefs can shape your dating patterns, often in ways that are not helpful. CBT helps lay the groundwork for healthier relationships by identifying and addressing these core beliefs.

Schemas: Understanding Relationship Patterns

Schemas are mental models that help us organize and make sense of information. Schemas can affect how we act when we're dating. For example, we might interpret silence as rejection or mistake jealousy for love. Unpacking and reshaping these schemas can result in interactions that are more balanced and satisfying.

A Path to Empowerment

It's like having a map for a trip to understand how CBT's basic ideas apply to dating. The cognitive triad, automatic thoughts, core beliefs, and schemas are the landmarks that show the way. The following sections will go into more detail about how CBT can be used in dating and offer concrete ways to improve.

Recognizing and Challenging Limiting Beliefs in Dating

Limiting beliefs can be like unwelcome passengers on our dating journey, whispering doubts in our ears and steering us off course. In this section, we'll discuss some of the most common limiting beliefs and how cognitive behavioral therapy (CBT) can help us deal with them.

Catastrophizing: Expecting the Worst

Catastrophizing in dating might look like assuming that one canceled date means the end of the relationship. It's that voice in your head that automatically draws the worst possible conclusion. He canceled our date, so this relationship is over.

CBT helps to recognize this pattern and challenge it with rational thinking. Is one canceled date really a catastrophe? Perhaps there's a logical explanation.

Filtering: Seeing Only the Negative

Filtering is concentrating only on the bad things and ignoring the good. Imagine going on a date and only remembering the awkward silence, not the laughter and shared interests. CBT tells us to look at the big picture, not just the parts that have been filtered and made to look bad.

Mind-Reading: Assuming You Know Others' Thoughts

How often have you assumed what your date is thinking?

"She's uninterested. I don't have enough appeal." Mind-reading can result in self-fulfilling prophecies. CBT helps us see that we can't really know what other people are thinking and encourages us to talk to them directly instead.

All-or-Nothing Thinking: It's Perfect or a Disaster

This belief can lead to thinking that a relationship is a failure if it isn't perfect. CBT helps us see the gray areas and understand that it's normal and healthy for relationships to experience ups and downs.

Emotional Reasoning: Feeling Equals Fact

"I feel unlovable, so I must be unlovable." Emotional reasoning confuses feelings with facts. By making a distinction between what we feel and what is true, CBT combats this. Feelings are real, but they don't always match what's going on in the world.

Should Statements: Imposing Rules on Ourselves

"By now, I should be married." "I should always know what to say on a date." These self-imposed rules can lead to unnecessary stress and disappointment. CBT helps us see and question these unrealistic expectations.

Overgeneralization:

Drawing broad conclusions from a single event. For instance, if one date goes poorly, believing that all future dates will be disasters. CBT encourages us to recognize that one event doesn't define a pattern.

Labeling:

Giving ourselves or others labels, such as "I'm a loser in love" or "All men/women are the same." CBT aids in our understanding of the complexity and individuality of each person, including ourselves.

Personalization:

Thinking that everything other people do or say is a response to us. If a date seems distracted, assume it's due to something you said or did. CBT makes us think about other explanations.

Magical Thinking:

Believing that if you think or wish for something, it will come true or has caused an event. "If I worry enough about this date, it will go well." CBT guides us to recognize that thoughts don't control outcomes.

Comparison Trap:

Comparing ourselves to others can make us feel bad or good about ourselves. CBT helps us see that comparisons aren't always fair and encourages self-acceptance.

Control Fallacies:

Thinking that you have no control over your life (external control) or that you must control every aspect of your life (internal control). CBT helps people find a middle ground between these two extremes.

Blame:

Blaming ourselves for things beyond our control or blaming others for our problems. CBT guides us in taking responsibility for what we can control and letting go of what we can't.

Fallacy of Change:

The fallacy of change is the idea that we can make other people change if we apply enough pressure or manipulation. CBT encourages us to see and respect the independence of others.

CBT in Action

Scenario 1: The Disastrous First Date

Scenario: Tom has been single for a while and finally asks someone out. The date goes poorly; there are awkward silences, and they don't seem to have much in common. He leaves feeling like a failure and thinks, "I'm terrible at dating. No one will ever like me."

Limiting Belief(s): Overgeneralization, Labeling

Reframe: "This date didn't go as well as I hoped, but it's just one experience. Not everyone will be a match, and that's okay. I'll learn from this and try again with someone else."

Scenario 2: The Comparison Trap

Scenario: Emily is excited about her new relationship but constantly compares it to her friends' relationships. She sees their social media posts and thinks, "They look so much happier than us. Something must be wrong with my relationship."

Limiting Belief(s): Comparison Trap

Reframe: "Every relationship is unique, and comparing mine to others' superficial social media images isn't fair or realistic. What matters is how my partner and I feel about each other."

Scenario 3: The Fear of Rejection

Scenario: James likes someone but is terrified to ask them out. He thinks, "They'll never say yes. I'm not good-looking or interesting enough. Why even try?"

Limiting Belief(s): Catastrophizing, Mind-reading, Labeling

Reframe: "I'm feeling nervous about asking them out, but I don't know what they'll say unless I try. I have qualities that others appreciate, and it's okay to give it a shot."

Scenario 4: The Control Fallacy

Scenario: Lisa's partner is going through a stressful time at work. Lisa feels that if she just does everything perfectly at home, her partner's stress will go away. She becomes overwhelmed trying to control everything.

Limiting Belief(s): Control Fallacies

Reframe: "I care about my partner and want to support them, but I can't control their work stress. I'll do what I can to be supportive, but I also need to take care of myself."

Scenario 5: The Magical Thinking in Long-term Relationships

Scenario: Mark and Sara are going through a rough patch. Mark believes that if he just wishes and hopes hard enough, things will get better. He avoids taking any concrete actions.

Limiting Belief(s): Magical Thinking

Reframe: "Wishing for things to improve isn't enough. We need to communicate, understand each other's needs, and take tangible steps to strengthen our relationship."

Creating a CBT plan for dating that is unique to you

When we have limiting beliefs and negative self-talk, dating can feel like an uphill battle. But what if we had a map that was just for us? Cognitive-behavioral therapy (CBT) gives us that map and empowers us to take charge of our dating lives. Here's how to make a CBT plan for dating that's just right for you:

1. Identify Your Specific Challenges

First, take some time to think about your dating experiences. What beliefs or actions have prevented you from moving forward? It could be a fear of being rejected, perfectionism, or envy. Be honest with yourself and write them down.

2. Understand Your Triggers

Consider the circumstances that lead to these unfavorable thoughts or actions next. Is it seeing a happy couple? Or maybe it's when a date doesn't go exactly as planned? Knowing your triggers enables you to plan ahead and respond appropriately.

3. Develop Positive Reframes

Now that you know your challenges and what sets them off, it's time to change the way you think about them. Create positive statements and thoughts to counter the negative ones using the techniques we discussed earlier.

For example:

"I'll never find someone," is a negative thought.

Reframe: *"I haven't found the right person yet, but I'm learning and growing with each experience."*

4. Practice Mindfulness and Self-Compassion

It's normal to feel angry or sad sometimes. Mindfulness and self-compassion can help you stay grounded. Give yourself the same kindness and patience you would show a friend.

5. Build Support Systems

If you need support, don't be afraid to lean on friends or a therapist. Professional assistance can sometimes give you the specific advice you need to get past a problem.

6. Constantly Improve and Adapt

Your CBT dating plan is dynamic. You change along with life. Review your plan on a regular basis, celebrate your wins, and make changes as necessary.

7. Seek Professional Help if Needed

Remember that it's okay to talk to a mental health professional if you're feeling stuck. Sometimes, we need an expert to help us see things from a different perspective.

Using a CBT journal to improve your dating life

A CBT journal can help with your dating life. Think of it as a personal coach, a confidante, and a record keeper all in one. Here are some reasons why it's good for you:

A Space for Reflection

Your CBT journal gives you a safe, private place to examine your thoughts, feelings, and actions. Writing down your thoughts after a date or even just an encounter gives you a chance to think back. What went well? What self-limiting ideas did you observe? How did you reframe them?

Tracking Your Progress

You can monitor your development over time by writing down your thoughts and reflections on a regular basis. You'll see how far you've come in challenging your limiting beliefs, recognizing triggers, and implementing positive reframes. This can be a very empowering and inspiring process.

Tool for Mindfulness

Your CBT journal promotes mindfulness. Taking the time to write allows you to stop and connect with your inner self. You become more aware of your thoughts and feelings, which helps you understand and take better care of yourself.

Creating a Customized Resource

As you write in it, your journal turns into a personalized resource full of ideas and tactics that work for you. You can go back to it for advice, ideas, or even just to remind yourself how strong and capable you are.

A Journey of Self-discovery

Dating isn't just about finding a partner; it's also about learning about yourself. You can explore your desires, values, and boundaries with the help of your CBT journal.

Encouragement for Ongoing Growth and Adaptation

It takes courage and self-love to start this CBT journey for dating. Recognizing your value and taking responsibility for your happiness is key. The road may be rough at times, but with dedication and fortitude, you'll get there.

By creating a customized CBT plan, you give yourself the tools you need to navigate the complicated world of dating with confidence and honesty. Accept the process, laugh at the twists and turns you didn't see coming, and never forget that you are deserving of love and happiness.

Keep this plan handy, review it often, and enjoy the adventure of dating as your true self. You've got this!

CHAPTER SEVEN

ANXIOUS ATTACHMENT IN LONG-TERM RELATIONSHIPS

Long-term relationships bring joy and comfort, but they also require hard work, trust, and communication, especially when anxious attachment comes into play. For couples where one or both partners experience anxious attachment, understanding this dance is crucial.

Some people might be surprised to learn that a relationship between two people who are anxiously attached can be successful in the context of anxious attachment. But it can, and I can tell you that from personal experience.

My wife and I, who have been married for 30-plus years, have both said that we are anxiously attached. Our early years were full of misunderstandings, strong feelings, and a need for reassurance that seemed to never end. Some people might see this as a recipe for disaster, but for us, it led to a deep understanding and connection.

We learned to recognize each other's triggers (for example, yelling at each other is a big no-no) and found ways to respond with empathy rather than anxiety. We agreed to communicate honestly and openly, always trying to understand rather than judge.

Our relationship has its ups and downs, but the anxious attachment that could have caused us to drift apart instead brought us closer together. We shared their fears, needs, and desires, so we understood them. Despite our anxious attachment, we were able to build trust.

This doesn't mean that our path was easy or that every relationship with an anxious attachment will go the same way. But our experience shows that an anxiously attached relationship can be strong, loving, and incredibly rewarding with work, understanding, and a willingness to grow together.

Our journey has taught us that love isn't about being perfect. Instead, it's about accepting flaws, getting stronger through hard times, and celebrating the special bond that brings two people together.

In many ways, our anxiously attached relationship has been our greatest teacher, guiding us toward a deeper understanding of ourselves, each other, and the beautiful complexity of love.

Anxious attachment feels like a wall between two loving partners. It's a perplexing combination of wanting closeness but being afraid of it, and wanting trust but finding it hard to build. These opposing feelings can make the dance of love feel like a tug of war, leaving both partners exhausted and unfulfilled.

But this doesn't mean that those who struggle with anxious attachment can't have a happy, healthy long-term relationship. Instead, it's an opportunity to grow, connect on a deeper level, and build a resilient, compassionate, and understanding relationship.

Building Trust

Any successful relationship is built on trust. It's what makes it possible for partners to feel safe, to open up, and to be vulnerable with one another. But for those with anxious attachment, trust can feel like an elusive, fragile thing.

Sarah and Tom are very in love but are having trouble with Sarah's anxious attachment. Sarah frequently doubts Tom's commitment due to her fears and insecurities. Tom, despite being patient, starts to feel overwhelmed as she requires constant reassurance.

They start a journey to rebuild trust through open communication, empathy, and a willingness to understand each other's needs. They create rituals of connection, set clear expectations, and, most importantly, promise to be there for each other.

Sarah learns to express her needs without letting fear take over, and Tom learns how to support Sarah without feeling trapped. Together, they make an environment where trust grows and their relationship grows.

Communication Techniques

The lifeline that keeps a relationship alive and well is communication, which goes hand in hand with trust. Communication becomes even more important in the context of anxious attachment.

Take the case of Michael and James, a couple who had to deal with James's anxious attachment. James's fear of abandonment frequently showed up as accusations and withdrawal, which left Michael confused and hurt.

They realized that their love for each other was too valuable to let misunderstandings ruin it. Together, they worked to find a way to talk that respected both their feelings and needs. They practiced active listening, used "I" statements to express feelings, and made a safe space for honest, nonjudgmental conversation.

Over time, this helped them connect on a deeper level, understanding each other's triggers and responding with empathy rather than defensiveness.

Recognizing and Handling Red Flags

Recognizing and addressing red flags is essential in long-term relationships. Red flags are warning signs that something might be wrong in a relationship. They might be signs of potential issues, deeper problems, or even danger. It's important to remember that not every red flag means a relationship is doomed, but they should prompt careful consideration and maybe even professional help. Here are some warning signs, especially for those with anxious attachment:

Excessive Jealousy or Possessiveness:

While some jealousy is normal, if a partner is constantly suspicious, accusatory, or controlling about a person's whereabouts and relationships with others, it can be a sign of deeper trust issues that may need to be addressed.

Ignoring Boundaries:

Ignoring or dismissing boundaries can cause a breakdown in trust and respect in the relationship. Examples include not respecting personal space, making decisions for the other person without asking, and constantly pushing past comfort zones.

Manipulative Behavior:

This includes things like using guilt, being passive-aggressive, or playing games to get what one wants. This kind of behavior can be especially upsetting for someone who suffers from anxious attachment, and it can also make it harder for two people to be honest and open with each other, which is important for a healthy relationship.

Verbal or Physical Abuse:

Any kind of abuse is a red flag and usually needs professional help. This can include insulting, yelling, calling names, or using any kind of physical force or intimidation.

Consistent Lack of Support or Validation:

If a partner ignores or downplays feelings, especially when it comes to anxiety or attachment issues, it can lead to resentment and confusion. Everyone needs help and reassurance, especially when they are going through difficult times.

Unresolved Past Traumas or Relationship Patterns:

If a partner brings unresolved pain or patterns from previous relationships into the current one without addressing or talking about them, it can show up as irrational behavior, overreactions, or unexplained anger or sadness.

Chronic Lying:

Repeatedly lying, even about small things, can undermine trust and make someone with anxious attachment feel even more insecure and afraid in the relationship.

Emotional Unavailability:

A partner who is consistently distant, uninterested, or dismissive of emotional needs might not be able or willing to provide the level of connection and reassurance that someone with anxious attachment might need.

Constant Criticism:

Constant criticism, whether it's about big or small things, can hurt a person's self-esteem and make the environment hostile.

Rushing Intimacy:

Moving too quickly into emotional or physical intimacy, pushing for commitment, or ignoring the natural pace of a relationship could be signs of desperation or insecurity.

Take Emily and Clara, who have been together for five years. Emily's anxious attachment has always been a part of their relationship, but Clara has recently noticed some worrying signs. Emily's need for reassurance has become an obsession, and her jealousy has gotten to the point where it's hard to breathe.

Clara recognizes these as warning signs and understands that they must be addressed. She doesn't ignore them or brush them off. Instead, she starts a gentle conversation with Emily and expresses her worries and desire to know what's going on.

THE NO-NONSENSE ANXIOUS ATTACHMENT BOOK

They decide to get professional help to find out what might be causing Emily's anxious attachment to get worse. Therapy gives them a place to work on these worries, learn new coping mechanisms, and strengthen their bond.

Recognizing warning signs is not about pointing fingers or finding faults. It's about caring enough about the relationship and each other to talk about what might be wrong before it gets worse. It's a sign of power, empathy, and dedication to the relationship's success.

Embracing the Journey

Anxious attachment doesn't have to mean relationship trouble for the rest of your life. Like any other challenge in love, it's an opportunity to grow, deepen understanding, and build something beautiful.

The stories of Sarah and Tom, Michael and James, and Emily and Clara show that love can grow even when there is anxious attachment present. It takes work, patience, and empathy, but the result is a connection that lasts, grows, and makes you happy.

Long-term relationships with anxious attachment are a dance that may stumble and falter at times, but with trust, communication, and a watchful eye for red flags, it can be graceful, passionate, and endlessly rewarding.

This chapter has taken us through the dynamics of building trust, crafting communication strategies, and dealing with red flags in the context of anxious attachment in long-term relationships. We've seen real-life examples, personal stories, and practical insights that paint a vivid picture of what it means to love and be loved with anxious attachment.

The journey may not be easy, but it's one worth taking, filled with lessons, growth, and the pure, profound joy of connecting deeply with another human being.

CHAPTER EIGHT

UNDERSTANDING THE FOUR ATTACHMENT STYLES AND THEIR INTERPLAY IN PERSONAL AND ROMANTIC RELATIONSHIPS

The Rich Tapestry of Attachment

Attachment is a world; it's not just a word. Attachment styles, which are as varied as human emotions, show how we bond, love, trust, and occasionally fight.

Understanding attachment is like finding the hidden rules of a complicated game we all play but were never taught the rules of. The various attachment styles aren't just ideas; they're real, living patterns that we all show in different ways. Recognizing them helps us navigate the maze of human connections.

The Four Main Attachment Styles

Secure Attachment

Causes:

Early childhood caregiving that is consistent, loving, and responsive is typically what leads to a secure attachment.

Behaviors:

Securely attached people are comfortable with closeness, can express their needs openly, and trust that others will respond favorably.

Relationships:

In a safe relationship, both people respect and understand each other.

· · · ●· ● · · ·

Anxious Attachment (also referred to as Preoccupied or Ambivalent)

Causes:

Confusion and insecurity can result from inconsistent or unpredictable caregiving, which can lead to an anxious attachment.

Behaviors:

People who are anxiously attached want closeness and affirmation but are afraid of rejection and abandonment, which makes them clingy or controlling.

Relationships:

Relationships with anxiously attached partners can feel intense and emotional, but they can also be tense and full of anxiety.

· · · ● · ● ● · ·

Avoidant Attachment (also referred to as Dismissive)

Causes:

Avoidant attachment is frequently caused by emotional neglect or unresponsive caregiving.

Behaviors:

Avoidantly attached people may avoid close relationships, act distant or dismissive, and value independence over connection.

Relationships:

Avoidant relationships may lack depth and emotional engagement, resulting in flimsy connections.

· · · ● · ● ● · ·

Disorganized Attachment (also referred to as Fearful-Avoidant)

Causes:

Traumatic or extremely stressful early experiences may cause disorganized attachment.

Behaviors:

People with disorganized attachment can act in strange, confusing ways, moving back and forth between being close and being far away.

Relationships:

Relationships that aren't well-organized are often unpredictable, full of conflict, and don't have a clear pattern of interaction.

We can see parts of ourselves and other people in these portraits of attachment. We start to see patterns and connections, and we start to see the invisible threads that connect us. But what happens when these styles collide? How do they fit together or clash, harmonize or clash? The next section will explore the dynamic dance between various attachment styles.

· · · ● · ● · ● · ·

Interactions Between Anxious and the Other Attachment Styles

Anxious with Anxious

When two anxiously attached people get together, it's like getting a double dose of intensity. A passionate but rocky relationship can result from the need for closeness, the fear of abandonment, and the emotional rollercoaster. Misunderstandings may quickly get worse, and reassuring words may never be enough.

Take the case of Jake and Emily, who are both anxiously attached. They fell in love quickly and deeply. Their connection was electric, but so was their anxiety. Small disagreements would turn into all-night arguments, and moments of doubt would snowball into crises. They wanted to trust each other but couldn't get past their own fears. It was a love that seemed fated but also doomed.

Secure with Anxious

A secure and anxiously attached relationship could help the anxious partner feel better. The secure person's ability to communicate openly, give consistent support, and not be threatened by the anxious partner's need for closeness can create a stable base.

Joanna, who was securely attached, met David, who was anxiously attached, at a friend's party. Joanna was initially unsure of David's fears and insecurities, but her steady and calm presence helped David open up. They developed a relationship in which David learned to trust and Joanna learned to understand. Despite their differences, they found harmony.

Avoidant and Anxious

The push-and-pull dance of avoidant and anxious attachment can be difficult. A cycle of miscommunication and frustration could result from the anxiously attached person's desire for closeness clashing with the avoidant partner's need for distance.

Michael, who was avoidantly attached, and Lisa, who was anxiously attached, had trouble finding their rhythm. Lisa's fears were sparked by Michael's withdrawal, and Lisa's neediness made Michael pull away even more. They loved each other, but they were lost in translation.

Other Combinations

A wide range of possibilities and traps are revealed when different attachment styles are combined. Secure with avoidant, anxious with disorganized, and all the other combinations each have their own dynamics, difficulties, and opportunities for growth.

These interactions are merely launching points; they do not determine fate. These patterns can be changed through awareness, communication, empathy, and a willingness to grow. The dance of attachment is ever-changing, but with understanding, we can learn to move with grace, wisdom, and connection.

Strategies for Navigating Attachment Dynamics

Understanding Yourself

Finding one's attachment style is like finding one's own road map to relationships. It's not about putting people in boxes or assigning blame; it's about understanding and accepting. Growth is possible from this place of awareness.

Alan spent many years moving from one bad relationship to the next. He didn't realize he was anxiously attached until he started to examine his attachment style with the aid of therapy. This realization was like a light bulb going off, showing patterns and opening up new ways to move forward.

Communicating Needs and Boundaries

In all relationships, but especially when dealing with different attachment styles, clear and compassionate communication is essential. Understanding and trust can be developed by being able to express needs and set limits.

Marcia, an avoidant attaché, had a hard time telling Eddie, an anxiously attached partner, that she needed space. Through open communication and a willingness to be vulnerable, they were able to find a balance that met both of their needs.

Seeking Professional Help if Needed

Without help, it can be hard to figure out how attachment styles interact. Therapists or counselors who have been trained in attachment theory can provide insights, tools, and support that are specifically suited to the needs of each person and their relationships.

James and Karen were in a never-ending cycle of fighting and miscommunication. With the help of a skilled therapist, they were able to identify their attachment patterns, communicate more effectively, and rebuild their relationship.

Investing in Personal Growth

A person's attachment style often limits their ability to grow. This can include self-care practices, learning new communication skills, engaging in hobbies or activities that build self-esteem, or connecting with supportive communities.

Olivia was sick of being ruled by her worries about relationships. She started to invest in herself by taking yoga classes, joining a support group, and reading books that fed her soul. Her relationships grew as she did.

Moving Forward Together

The journey of exploring and navigating attachment styles is deeply personal, but it is also universal. We all want to connect and be understood, to love and be loved. We can construct bridges rather than walls by accepting our own and others' complexity.

We'll keep delving deeper into topics like relationships at work, parenting, and coping mechanisms in the chapters that follow. Understanding human connection is a rich, multi-layered, and never-ending adventure. Ready to learn more?

CHAPTER NINE

ANXIOUS ATTACHMENT AND THE WORKPLACE

For many of us, work is more than just a paycheck. It's where we spend a big chunk of our lives, make friends, and try to improve ourselves both personally and professionally. But what happens when the underlying currents of anxious attachment enter the seemingly straightforward domain of professional relationships?

Understanding Anxious Attachment in a Professional Context

Our personal lives are not the only ones affected by anxious attachment. It can seep into our work lives and change how we interact with coworkers, bosses, and even clients. Even though the rules at work are different from those at home, the emotions, fears, and patterns that underlie anxious attachment are still the same.

An excessive need for approval from bosses or coworkers can be a sign of anxious attachment in the workplace. It could lead to a constant need for reassurance about performance, difficulty accepting constructive criticism, or even a tendency to hold on to relationships at work that might not be healthy.

But why should we care about anxious attachment at work? It's not just a matter of individual preferences or quirks. Work performance, team dynamics, and individual well-being are all impacted by this issue.

The Relevance of Anxious Attachment to Work Relationships

The way we interact with others at work affects not only how happy we are with our jobs, but also how our careers will go. An individual with anxious attachment may be held back by fears and insecurities that are not necessarily related to their actual skills or abilities.

For example, if you have anxious attachment, you might worry too much about how other people see you because you're afraid of being rejected or judged. This can make you afraid to take risks, speak up in meetings, or look for new opportunities, even if you're fully capable.

The flip side? Understanding and recognizing anxious attachment at work can help you grow as a person and improve your relationships. It's not about changing who you are, but about figuring out how these feelings affect how you interact with others at work.

Anxious Attachment with Coworkers: A Delicate Balance

Building friendships with coworkers is a natural and often rewarding part of our professional lives. These friendships can make working long hours more fun and help people feel like they're part of a team. The dynamics, however, can sometimes become more complicated and problematic when anxious attachment is added to the mix.

The Coworker as a Confidante

Consider yourself a member of a close-knit team. You share jokes, lunch breaks, and maybe even some personal stories. It can feel safe and welcoming. But for someone with anxious attachment, the line between friendship and dependence can get blurry.

For example, let's look at a situation in which Melissa, a hard-working professional, becomes close to Trevor, a coworker. They frequently have lunch together and work on projects together. It's a happy relationship until Melissa starts to worry about a promotion she wants. She frequently asks Trevor for advice on her work and seeks constant reassurance from him. Trevor's initial help turns into discomfort as he feels overwhelmed by her neediness.

This isn't unusual, and it's not always wrong or bad. However, it does show how anxious attachment can turn a good working relationship into one that is unbalanced and tense.

The Coworker as a Rival

Clinginess and overdependence are not the only signs of anxious attachment. Sometimes it's the complete opposite. It can lead to competition, jealousy, or even hostility, especially when it comes to people who work in the same industry.

Consider Francisco, who gets more and more jealous of his coworker Cathy as she receives praise for her accomplishments. Francisco sees Cathy as a threat rather than a peer because his anxious attachment makes him feel inadequate. His interactions with her become bitter, which hurts not only their relationship but also the way the team functions as a whole.

Strategies for Balance

The workplace is a microcosm of all the different ways people interact with one another. The first step in achieving balance is to recognize the symptoms of anxious attachment and comprehend how it might affect professional relationships.

Open communication, setting boundaries, and seeking feedback can go a long way in navigating the delicate dance of coworker relationships when anxious attachment is involved. It's about being aware of your own triggers and the comfort levels of others, and trying to build relationships that are supportive but not suffocating.

Coworker attachment anxiety doesn't have to be a barrier. It can be an opportunity to grow, learn, and strengthen connections, just like your long and happy marriage.

Navigating Power Dynamics in Anxious Attachment to Bosses

For those who suffer from anxious attachment, professional relationships with bosses can be complicated. The power dynamic between a boss and an employee can make the employee feel insecure, needy, or even angry.

Seeking Approval

Anxiously attached people might worry too much about getting their boss's approval. The need for approval can consume all of your time. Consider Daniel, a young marketing expert who is determined to impress his new manager, Perla. Perla appreciates Daniel's enthusiasm, but she soon realizes that his constant need for feedback and reassurance is taking up a lot of her time. Daniel's worries about approval cause him to doubt his own skills, which turns into a self-fulfilling prophecy of doubt.

Fear of Confrontation

Anxiously attached people, on the other hand, might try too hard to avoid conflict with their supervisor. This can result in suppressed feelings, a lack of assertiveness, and, ultimately, dissatisfaction at work.

Consider Laura, a seasoned project manager who has trouble telling her boss, Richard, what she thinks. Richard frequently makes changes at the last minute that affect the whole team, but Laura never brings it up because she doesn't want to get into a fight. Her worries hold her back, which frustrates both her and her coworkers.

Striking a Balance

When anxious attachment is present, navigating the complex dynamics with a boss can be difficult but not impossible. Here are some things you can do to help:

Knowing Your Triggers:

Recognize the situations or behaviors that can make your anxious attachment worse. Is it criticism, a lack of feedback, or something else? You can deal with these triggers in a proactive manner by identifying them.

Setting Boundaries:

Don't be afraid to talk to your boss about your expectations. Instead of constantly seeking reassurance, ask for feedback in a structured way. If confrontation is hard for you, practice assertive communication techniques.

Seeking Support:

If your relationship with your boss gets tense because of anxious attachment, don't be afraid to ask for professional help or a mentor within the company. Sometimes, getting ideas and strategies from someone outside the situation can be very helpful.

Remember that professional growth is a process, not a goal. Your relationship with your boss is just one part of your career, and it can be very helpful to understand how anxious attachment affects that relationship.

Creating a Supportive Workplace Culture: An Anxious Attachment Perspective

Anxiously attached people often have problems with their relationships at work, but these problems don't define their whole professional experience. A supportive workplace culture that understands and accommodates anxious attachment can be developed by employers, managers, and employees alike.

Emphasizing Empathy

In the workplace, empathy can be a game-changer. An environment where empathy is not only encouraged but also actively practiced may provide the support anxiously attached people need to thrive.

Think about a company that regularly puts on team-building events that emphasize emotional intelligence. These kinds of activities can break down barriers, increase understanding, and make the workplace a more caring place where everyone feels seen and valued.

Encouraging Communication

For any successful working relationship, clear and open communication is essential, especially for those who struggle with anxious attachment. Building communication skills across an organization helps make it a place where people can trust one another and feel less worried and uncertain.

A company that offers communication workshops or open channels for feedback fosters a culture where everyone can express their thoughts and concerns without fear of judgment or retaliation.

Flexibility and Accommodation

Being flexible is essential because anxious attachment can affect people in different ways. Anxiously attached people can discover what works best for them by giving them options for different working styles or encouraging personalized approaches.

For example, allowing flexible work hours, remote working options, or personalized project management can make a big difference in the overall happiness and productivity of an anxiously attached employee.

The Role of Leadership

A supportive workplace culture depends heavily on leadership. Leaders who understand the value of mental health and relationships are more likely to create a place where anxiously attached people can grow and succeed.

Leaders can make a good workplace culture that recognizes and supports different attachment styles by setting an example, fostering collaboration, and encouraging personal growth.

Building Relationships That Work

Relationships at work can be complicated, especially when anxious attachment is involved. But with awareness, empathy, communication, and flexibility, it is possible to create a workplace where everyone can succeed.

Your own experiences in both personal and professional relationships can show the power of understanding, empathy, and growth. By recognizing the unique challenges and opportunities that anxious attachment presents, workplaces can become more welcoming, compassionate, and effective for everyone.

CHAPTER TEN

PARENTING AND ANXIOUS ATTACHMENT

Parenting is an exciting adventure full of joy, wonder, challenges, and unknowns. For parents with anxious attachment, this adventure takes on new dimensions. The intertwining threads of affection, worry, connection, and anxiety create a special fabric that defines the family's relationships.

Anxious attachment in parents is similar to an overzealous dance partner who sometimes moves too quickly or hesitates out of doubt. It's a good thing to want to connect, protect, and care for others, but it can be overwhelming at times. But what does this mean for the child growing up in a parent's loving but worried arms?

As a father who has been married for more than 30 years and has an anxious attachment to my wife, I know firsthand how hard it is to find the right balance when raising children. It's a dance in which both partners must learn to lead and follow, sometimes stepping on each other's toes but always aiming for harmony.

A complex relationship with subtleties and big implications exists between parenting styles and anxious attachment. It's not just worry or overprotection. A child's life can be profoundly shaped by this multifaceted emotional experience.

Through the lens of anxious attachment, this chapter will examine the complexities of parenting. Together, we'll look at the factors, effects, tactics, and chances for development that come up when anxiety and parenting collide. It is a journey of understanding, compassion, and empowerment that starts with recognizing the long-term effects on children's development.

But first, let's look at what anxious attachment really means and how it ties into the sacred role of parenting.

Influence of Anxious Attachment on Children's Development

Attachment forms in the parent-child relationship. It is a reflection of how the parent was raised, a complicated interaction of feelings, actions, expectations, and wants. Anxiously attached parents bring their fears, hopes, and dreams from their past into their parenting journey.

Imagine a parent standing at the school gates, heart pounding as they watch their child enter a new world. This isn't just a worry about getting hurt or doing poorly in school. It's a profound emotional experience that gets to the heart of who they are.

As a parent who also experiences anxious attachment, I know how easy it is to let your fears control what you do. In my own life, I have hovered, questioned, and second-guessed myself. I've had the urge to protect, even when it might not have been necessary. It's a hard balance to find, and you need to be self-aware, have empathy, and keep growing.

But anxious attachment is not a barrier to good parenting; rather, it's a landscape full of insights, possibilities, and chances for close connection.

Influence on Children's Development

The child's life is affected by anxious attachment, not just the parent's. Children of anxiously attached parents may learn to look at the world with caution, hesitation, or uncertainty.

But they also learn to get around in the world by being very aware of their emotions, empathy, and connections. The intense focus on feelings, needs, and relationships of an anxiously attached parent can help their children develop emotional intelligence and resilience.

This shows how important it is to understand the dynamics of anxious attachment in parenting. It's not a universal experience, nor is it a set pattern that can't be changed.

Parenting Styles and Their Impact

The parenting style adopted by an anxiously attached parent can have a big impact on how the parent and child interact. Let's look at different parenting methods and how they work in this situation.

1. Authoritarian Parenting Style

Without much warmth or nurturing, an authoritarian parent demands obedience and conformity. When coupled with an anxious attachment, this can lead to a strong fear of disappointing the parent. The child may develop an excessive dependence on external approval and have trouble with self-confidence.

For example, I remember times in our home when my worries manifested as a need for control. I would be overly strict with homework or chores because I was afraid that a mistake would make my child look bad. It took time and self-reflection to realize that my fears were driving this behavior and that what my child really needed was understanding and encouragement.

2. Permissive Parenting Style

Permissive parenting is characterized by high warmth but low expectations and discipline. An anxiously attached parent may use this style to make up for their own fears and insecurities. The child may feel loved and cared for, but he or she may also have trouble setting limits and exercising self-control.

In my own experience, there were times when I was so afraid of disappointing my child that I gave in to every request, even when I knew it wasn't in his or her best interest. Finding the right amount of help without being too controlling was a delicate balance.

3. Authoritative Parenting Style

The authoritative parenting style is often thought to be the most balanced because it combines warmth and understanding with clear expectations and boundaries. An anxiously attached parent who adopts this style may find a healthy middle ground by encouraging their child's independence while also offering loving support.

My wife and I found this method to be the most helpful in our parenting journey. It helped us recognize our own worries without letting them control how we raised our children. We worked hard to make sure our kids felt seen and heard while also learning the importance of responsibility and self-discipline.

4. Neglectful or Uninvolved Parenting Style

Neglectful or uninvolved parenting, characterized by low warmth and low expectations, can be especially harmful when combined with anxious attachment. The child may feel abandoned and unsupported as a result of the parent's fears and insecurities making them withdraw.

Although this was never how we raised our kids, we saw what happened when friends didn't take care of their kids. The parents' worries turned inward, leaving the child to deal with their emotions on their own.

Building Trust with Your Child

Building trust with your child is like building a bridge across a river of feelings and experiences. It's a delicate process that takes time, patience, and a willingness to be open. Trust is both a challenge and an opportunity for parents who struggle with anxious attachment.

Self-awareness is the first step toward trust. Parents who are anxiously attached need to be aware of their own triggers and patterns and understand how their attachment style affects how they interact with their kids. This isn't about pointing fingers or feeling bad; it's about learning and improving.

As a father of three, I've experienced the conflict between my own worries and what my kids need. I remember the small things, like holding my daughter's hand as she took her first steps and feeling both excited and nervous. And the big ones, like seeing my sons leave for college in a whirlwind of pride, hope, and fear.

These are the things that weave the fabric of trust. They are the things you've done together, the honest conversations you've had, and your willingness to listen, learn, and change.

Building trust also means giving your child a safe place where they know they are seen, heard, and valued. It means respecting boundaries, even if those boundaries push against your own fears.

It's an art form, a delicate balance of giving and taking, leading and following, holding on and letting go.

Trust develops over time. Through regular, loving interaction, it develops layer by layer. And for anxiously attached parents, it's a journey worth taking, a path that leads to a deeper connection, richer understanding, and a loving, supportive relationship that will last.

Influence on Children's Development

The years of childhood are a time of rapid growth and change, when the habits, beliefs, and relationships of the future are formed. As a parent with anxious attachment, you have a profound and complex impact on your child's development.

It starts with the emotional atmosphere you create. Children are keen observers, picking up on the subtleties of your reactions, your voice tone, and your body language. Your interactions with them teach them about trust, safety, and connection.

A child's development can be impacted in many different ways by anxious attachment. It can cause increased sensitivity to rejection or criticism, a propensity to internalize stress, and a strong desire to please others. It can also help people develop empathy, fortitude, and a keen awareness of how others feel.

As I watched my own kids deal with friendships, sports, and school, I recognized signs of my own worries in their actions. My son used to worry excessively about his grades, so we sat down and talked about what was making him so worried. It led to a more in-depth discussion about expectations, success, and self-worth.

The journey wasn't always easy. There were bumps and detours, moments of misunderstanding, and chances for growth. But through it all, we learned to get by working together and finding ways to help each other grow.

For parents with anxious attachment, it's important to understand that your attachment style is not set in stone. It is a place to start, a framework that can be understood, looked into, and even changed.

A positive and nurturing environment can be created by first understanding how your attachment style affects your child's development. It means being aware of your reactions, trying to understand what your child needs, and finding ways to connect that respect both your and their experiences.

It's a difficult but rewarding journey that leads to more compassion, understanding, and connections.

CHAPTER ELEVEN

STORIES OF HOPE AND SUCCESS

Rebecca's Transformation: A Path from Fear to Freedom

Rebecca was born in Wisconsin, in a small town called Milford that is tucked between rolling hills and sparkling lakes. Her father, a middle school teacher, was the epitome of dedication but struggled with anxious attachment. Her mother, a nurse, was the calming force in their family but often bore the brunt of her husband's fears and insecurities.

Rebecca loved to paint when she was younger. She was able to express feelings she couldn't put into words thanks to the vibrant colors and brush strokes. She did well in her art classes, but schoolwork was always hard for her, especially when her anxious tendencies started to show.

As a teenager, she found comfort in her friends, but her need to be reassured all the time caused problems. Rebecca's constant need for approval frequently overwhelmed Emily, her best friend.

Rebecca's transition to college was both exciting and terrifying. She moved to Chicago to study Art History at Northwestern University. The noise and chaos of the big city were both exciting and terrifying. She fell in love with Michael, a fellow student who was a charming Literature major who loved poetry.

Their relationship began beautifully, with romantic walks and shared dreams. But Rebecca's anxious attachment started to show. She would anxiously wait for Michael's texts, try to decipher what he meant, and worry if he was ever late for a date. Her jealousy over his friendships with other women became a constant issue.

Rebecca's life fell apart when they broke up. She was in her tiny apartment, surrounded by canvases and brushes, but she couldn't paint. Her grades went down, and she felt lost and alone.

She made the decision to go to therapy after that. Rebecca's mentor on the path to self-discovery was an attachment disorder expert. Together, they talked about Rebecca's childhood memories, broke down her relationship with her parents, and figured out what was making her anxious attachment.

Rebecca's sessions with her therapist were full of tears and revelations. She learned to recognize her triggers, such as her father's voice tone or the way Michael looked at his watch. Her therapist taught her mindfulness exercises, which helped her pay attention to her breath, feel the texture of her paintbrush, and be in the present moment.

Rebecca started to recover gradually. She got a job at a nearby art gallery, where she got to do what she loved for a living while doing what she loved. She joined a painting group and made friends with people who shared her passion without carrying the weight of her past anxieties.

She met Tom, a graphic designer with a kind spirit and an understanding heart. Their relationship was unique because it was based on trust and open communication. They married in a small ceremony by the lake in Milford, they were joined by family and friends who had seen Rebecca change.

Rebecca's story is one of fortitude, self-awareness, and development. From the quiet streets of Milford to the busy center of Chicago, her journey from fear to freedom is a vivid, real-life example of overcoming anxious attachment.

· · · ● · ● · ● · ·

From Boardroom Battles to Inner Balance: Mark's Path to Harmony

Mark's life was a whirlwind of business meetings, sales goals, and flights. He was born in Austin, Texas, and worked his way up the corporate ladder in the tech industry. His mother, a stay-at-home mom, helped him develop a softer side, though Mark rarely showed it. His father, a retired Army Colonel, instilled in him a strong sense of discipline.

Lisa, a lively woman with a love for helping others, was Mark's college sweetheart. They had two children, Emily and Ethan, and moved to a beautiful house in San Francisco. On the surface, life seemed perfect, but Mark's anxious attachment cast a cloud over their family.

Mark was consumed by work. Failure terrified him like a monster that was always after him. A stern look from his boss or a casual remark from a coworker could send him into a panic. He was constantly asking Lisa for reassurance at home because he was worried about their money, their kids' education, and the stability of their relationship.

Lisa got tired of Mark's constant worrying. Family dinners were overshadowed by Mark's work calls and emails, and the romantic getaways turned into stressful trips.

The turning point came when Mark lost his job during a company restructuring. His worst fears came true, and the ground beneath him seemed to disappear. He found himself unable to sleep, eat, or enjoy life as a result of his anxiety.

But Mark chose to put himself back together rather than fall apart. He joined a local group for people with anxiety, where he met people from all walks of life who were all dealing with similar problems. He could relate to what they were saying, and for the first time, he felt understood.

Mark began to examine his anxious attachment with the help of a caring therapist. His mother's quiet suffering and his father's strict expectations were the causes. He learned to identify his emotional triggers and came up with coping mechanisms like journaling and meditation.

The rift between Mark and his family started to mend. He spent more time with Emily and Ethan, rediscovering the joy of simple things like playing catch in the yard and baking cookies. He and Lisa fell in love again, and they talked about their hopes and dreams.

Mark got a new job, this time with a non-profit group that supports education. It was a change from the cutthroat corporate world, but it fit with his newfound values. His anxieties no longer controlled him, and the work was satisfying.

From the chaos of the boardroom to inner peace was not an easy or quick journey. It was a winding road with both setbacks and victories. But Mark's change is a testament to the strength of self-awareness, therapy, and the human spirit.

He still experiences anxiety, but it no longer defines him. His story is an uplifting tapestry of personal growth that gives hope to people who are struggling with anxious attachment in their personal and professional lives.

· · · · ● · ● · · ·

Sam and Oliver: Healing Through Love and Understanding

Sam, a compassionate therapist with years of experience, never thought she would find herself navigating the tricky waters of anxious attachment in her personal life. Oliver, an introspective and struggling writer, dealt with anxious attachment from his early years, always fearing abandonment and craving reassurance.

When they first met at a mutual friend's art gallery, the attraction was undeniable. Sam was drawn to Oliver's depth, his passion for words, and his vulnerable honesty. Oliver found solace in Sam's understanding nature, feeling an instant connection with someone who seemed to truly see him.

However, the early days of romance quickly gave way to Oliver's insecurities. Jealousy reared its ugly head when Sam spent time with her male friends, and neediness crept in when Oliver required constant reassurance of Sam's love and commitment. The more he needed, the more Sam felt cornered, her professional knowledge of mental health a double-edged sword.

They had their highs and lows, moments of bliss followed by days of turmoil. Oliver's writing became a battlefield for his emotions, filled with eloquent expressions of love and stark confessions of fear. Sam found herself torn between her love for Oliver and the emotional toll his attachment style was taking on her.

Yet, they both knew there was something precious there, something worth fighting for. They decided to attend couples therapy, a decision that brought new challenges and revelations. It was a path neither smooth nor straightforward, filled with moments of realization, tears, laughter, and, most importantly, growth.

Oliver began to understand the roots of his anxious attachment, tracing them back to a tumultuous childhood where love was unpredictable and conditional. He started to see how those early patterns had shaped his relationships and self-perception.

Sam discovered her role in their dance of attachment, recognizing that her professional experience did not exempt her from personal blind spots. Together, they learned to communicate openly, to express needs without demands, to set boundaries, and to practice patience and empathy.

The journey wasn't easy, and there were times when both wondered if they should end it. But their commitment to each other, their shared values, and their determination to grow kept them moving forward. Slowly, they began to build a relationship that was stronger, healthier, more resilient.

Through time, effort, and a genuine willingness to change, they crafted a loving partnership that acknowledged Oliver's anxious attachment but refused to let it define them. They learned to appreciate each other's strengths, support one another in weaknesses, and create a bond that thrived on understanding, patience, and trust.

Today, they stand as a testament to the power of love, self-awareness, and commitment. Oliver's writing flourishes, filled with the richness of a life lived authentically. Sam continues to help others, enriched by her personal experience and deepened empathy.

Sam and Oliver's story is a beacon of hope for those struggling with anxious attachment, a real-life example that love, growth, and connection are not only possible but within reach. It reminds us that we are not defined by our fears or insecurities but by our ability to face them, learn from them, and rise above them.

• • • ● • ● • • •

Carol: From Fear to Freedom - The Solo Journey

Her anxious attachment had always been the main thing in Carol's life. She grew up in the busy city of Seattle with a single mother who had to work more than one job to make ends meet. Carol's father left when she was very young, and the void he left behind seemed to grow with her, turning into a haunting fear of being left alone.

She took this fear into her adult relationships, where she was always looking for confirmation and reassurance. She held on to partners tightly because she was afraid they would leave her like her father did. Again and again, she started relationships with a lot of passion and intensity, but they ended because of her insecurities.

But Carol was more than just her worry. She was a smart software engineer who loved classical music, read a lot, and cooked well. Her friends thought she was smart, funny, and a great cook who could make even the simplest ingredients into masterpieces.

After going through another painful breakup, Carol knew she had to do something different. The pattern was too clear, and she could no longer ignore the role her anxious attachment was playing in her life.

She decided to go on a trip by herself to learn more about herself. This trip would take her out of her comfort zone and force her to face her fears. She took a break from her job to travel through Europe, which was a place she had always wanted to see.

Her journey started out with a lot of doubt and fear. It was scary to be in a place she didn't know, to be alone, and to have no safety net. But as the days turned into weeks, she started to feel like something was changing.

She found out she was strong and tougher than she thought. She made friends with other travelers and locals, learned about art, history, and culture, and enjoyed simple things like a good cup of coffee or a beautiful sunset.

She kept a journal of what she did, what she thought, what scared her, and what she was proud of. She went to therapy online, where she got help and advice as she looked into the roots of her attachment problems.

Slowly, she started to realize that her worth did not depend on what other people thought of her and that she could be whole and complete on her own. She learned to trust herself, to love her independence, and to see that her anxious attachment was a part of her but not all of her.

Her journey took six months, but the change will last for the rest of her life. Carol didn't come back home as a completely different person, but as a more true version of herself. She brought back more than just memories and trinkets. She also brought back wisdom, self-love, and the freedom from her fears.

Carol still does well in her job, her relationships, and her life as a whole. Her story is not about a love story from a fairy tale. Instead, it is about a deep, personal love she has for herself. It shows how powerful self-discovery and courage can be, and how the human spirit can grow and heal.

Carol's story shows us that sometimes the most important relationship we need to fix is the one we have with ourselves. It's a story about hope, growth, and the amazing power we all have to move beyond our pasts and create a future full of joy, fulfillment, and honesty.

· · · ● · ● · · ·

Alex: Breaking Barriers and Building Bridges

Alex had always felt like an outsider, even though they were born in the heart of San Francisco's diverse and lively community. They struggled with their gender identity from a young age, feeling stuck in a body that didn't match who they were on the inside. This struggle happened on the inside, and it showed up as anxiety, depression, and a desperate need to connect and be understood.

An anxious attachment style seemed to be present in all of their relationships, which made their emotional lives even more complicated. Alex always felt insecure, needy, and afraid of being left alone, whether it was with friends, family, or romantic partners.

In many ways, their anxious attachment was a reflection of their journey to figure out who they were as a non-binary person. Fear of being rejected, judged, or left alone kept them from making deep, meaningful connections.

Alex was strong, brave, and determined to find acceptance and love, not just from other people but also from within. They cared deeply about human rights, were good at writing, and fought for LGBTQ+ causes. Their words struck a chord with a lot of people, and through writing, they were able to connect with people who understood their struggles and dreams.

Alex's life really changed when they met Jordan, a therapist who was openly gay and who specialized in LGBTQ+ mental health issues. Alex found hope in Jordan's ability to understand, care about, and give professional advice. Alex started to figure out what was behind their anxious attachment and the fears that drove it in therapy.

Jordan helped Alex see that their anxious attachment was not a flaw, but a natural reaction to a world that had often felt confusing and unwelcoming. Together, they came up with ways to boost Alex's self-confidence, help him accept himself, and set up a support system that celebrated his uniqueness.

They also looked at Alex's relationships and found warning signs, barriers to communication, and places where he could improve. Alex learned to value themselves, to ask for respect, and to set limits that took their needs and feelings into account.

Alex found a voice, an identity, and a sense of belonging that went beyond gender norms and societal expectations through this therapeutic journey. They started getting involved with the LGBTQ+ community by volunteering for groups, going to support groups, and becoming a source of hope for people who felt lost and alone.

Alex's story isn't just about getting over anxious attachment. It's also about breaking down walls, building bridges, and realizing the power of being yourself. It's a story that shows how different people's lives can be and how empathy, understanding, and self-love can change things.

In the end, Alex found a partner who accepted them for who they were and loved them for it. They found friends who helped and encouraged them, a community that understood them, and, most importantly, a self that they could love and be proud of.

Their story shows how acceptance can heal, how strength comes from being vulnerable, and how the need to connect is something we all have, no matter our gender, sexuality, or background. It's a reminder that everyone's journey is different, but that we all walk the same path toward self-discovery, growth, and love.

CHAPTER TWELVE

PART III: COPING MECHANISMS AND HEALING STRATEGIES

PRACTICAL STEPS TO OVERCOME ANXIETY ATTACHMENT

Living with Anxious Attachment

In the journey of understanding anxious attachment, we've explored its facets from relationships to parenting, and from the workplace to personal growth. Now, it's time to wrap it all together and look at what it means to live with anxious attachment on a daily basis. Acknowledging that certain advice may resonate across different contexts, this chapter offers a unique perspective, focusing on how to blend the insights and coping strategies into daily routines and life events. Whether you're an early bird greeting the sunrise or a night owl who finds solace in the midnight air, this chapter is dedicated to embracing anxious attachment as a part of your everyday existence. After all, living with anxious attachment isn't a full-stop sentence; it's merely a comma in the complex and beautiful narrative of life.

Creating a Balanced Daily Routine

Life is full of ordinary moments that can turn into amazing chances to learn and grow. Putting together a balanced daily routine that takes into account the specifics of anxious attachment can make the everyday more meaningful.

Morning Rituals

Imagine starting your day with awareness and intention. Setting the mood can be as easy as meditating or writing in a journal for five minutes. Think about how you feel, accept your worries, and tell yourself that they don't define you. Add one or two daily affirmations, such as "I am not my anxiety; I am strong and capable." Who says you can't cheer on yourself?

Work-Life Boundaries

Anxious attachment can sneak up on you on the way to the office or as you wander to your home office. Make it clear where your work life ends and your personal life begins. If you get a stressful email from your boss at 10 PM, tell yourself, "Work can wait, but my peace can't." Remember that even superheroes sometimes take off their capes.

Evening Reflections

The busyness of the day often leaves no time to think. A peaceful way to end the day is to have a nightly ritual where you think about the people you met, how you felt, and how you dealt with those things. A growth and acceptance mindset can be developed by keeping a gratitude journal or just making a mental note of what went well.

Integrating Anxious Attachment into Social Dynamics

When it comes to navigating the social whirlwind, anxious attachment might as well have a season pass. But don't worry, it's all part of the game. Here's how to play it well.

Friends and Get-togethers

We all have that friend who sends a text that says, "Are you mad at me?" if you don't answer within five minutes. Join the club if that's you. Friendships can feel like an emotional roller coaster when there is a lot of anxious attachment. What, though? When you know how to ride them, roller coasters are fun.

Take a moment the next time you're at a social event and start to feel nervous. Accept what's going on and let yourself have fun at the party. Try to talk to people without worrying about being judged or left behind. And, hey, no one said you couldn't sneak away to the snack table and talk to the cheese platter if you need a break.

Family Dynamics

Families are like a box of chocolates: you never know what you'll get. Anxious about being close to family? It's like biting into a bar of chocolate with a strange jelly center. It's unexpected and can be a little scary.

The key is to talk to each other. If something a family member does makes you feel anxious, talk about it. At first, it might feel awkward, like dancing the tango with two left feet, but with practice, you'll be gliding across the dance floor of family relationships.

Accepting Anxious Attachment in Romantic Relationships

Love… A many-splendored thing and a battlefield, especially when anxious attachment is a third wheel on your romantic date nights. But who says that three's a crowd? Here's how to make room for love, even if you're still worried about something.

Date Nights

Meeting someone new for a date? Are you anxiously attached? Welcome to the exciting ride that is the dating game. But don't worry, because you can handle it.

Recognize how you feel before the date. Maybe even have a little fun with them. "Oh, you again? Trying to convince me my date will stand me up? Nice try, but I'm still putting on my lucky socks."

Be present during the date. If anxiety comes to your door, ask it nicely to wait outside. Pay attention to the person, the conversation, and how you can help them. What if things go wrong? Remember that not every date will be your soulmate, and that's okay. Like a bad haircut, a bad date gets better over time.

Long-term Relationships

Anxious attachment can feel like a nosy neighbor who is always looking in through the window in a long-term relationship. But here's the secret: the curtains can be closed.

Tell your partner how you really feel. Talk about your triggers and what you can do together to make the environment safe and loving. It takes teamwork, like putting together IKEA furniture. It can be frustrating at times, but it's worth it in the end.

Attachment anxiety doesn't have to be the biggest problem. By recognizing it, understanding it, and finding ways to deal with it every day, it can become a part of your beautiful, multifaceted self that you can accept and manage. And just like that weird chocolate with jelly inside, you might even come to like it.

Anxious Attachment as a Path to Self-Discovery

What's crazy? Realizing that your anxious attachment isn't just a bothersome guest at the party, but a wise old friend who might be able to teach you a thing or two about yourself.

Anxiety Transformed Into Awareness

Anxiety may seem like an unwelcome party guest who stays too long, but it's more like a well-meaning neighbor who is just a little too enthusiastic. That neighbor might have a habit of knocking on your door at the worst times, but what if they're trying to tell you something important?

Your anxiety isn't just knocking; it's talking to you. It could be telling you about unspoken fears, desires, or something you need to deal with. It could be a warning about a relationship that doesn't feel right, or it could be a sign that you need to look into a certain area of your life. Listen to that knocking, invite it in for tea, and have a good old chat. You might learn something important about yourself.

Making Peace with Yourself

Anxious attachment need not be the bad guy in your life. It could be a peculiar sidekick that you need to learn more about. This isn't about changing who you are, but about accepting and learning from it.

Imagine that you are the captain of a ship, and that a crew member with anxious attachment is someone who occasionally feels scared. You wouldn't throw them overboard; instead, you'd figure out what makes them nervous and work with them to make the trip easier. Be the kind leader of your own life.

Self-Growth Through Connection

As you connect with your anxious attachment, you'll notice something beautiful happening. It won't be the enemy, but a guide. A roadmap for personal development, deeper connections, and a deeper understanding of yourself.

Ever heard the saying, "Keep your friends close and your enemies closer?" Anxious attachment might just be the frenemy who becomes a friend.

CHAPTER THIRTEEN

COPING MECHANISMS FOR RELATIONSHIPS

Embarking on the Journey

The most important journeys in life frequently start inside. Our relationships, whether they are happy or difficult, are based on how we feel about ourselves. The journey we'll take in this chapter won't take us to faraway lands or strange places, but rather to the deepest parts of our hearts and minds. Here, we'll look at the hidden paths that connect love and freedom, the compass of self-compassion, the oasis of mindfulness, and the bridges that build our sense of self.

For many of us, love and freedom may seem like competing forces. But in reality, they dance together, tangled up in a delicate balance that lets us experience relationships in all their richness. And like any good dance, getting the steps just right takes practice, awareness, and sometimes a little help.

The Path to Balancing Love and Freedom

Our first stop is the well-traveled path between love and freedom. It's a path full of misunderstandings, doubts, and occasionally fear. Finding the right balance between love and freedom can feel like trying to walk a tightrope, especially when our hearts are involved.

Consider Belinda and Jason as an example. Belinda, who called herself a "hopeless romantic," was known for jumping into relationships with both feet. Jason, on the other hand, prioritized his independence. When they first started dating, their differences became more obvious, which led to a lot of fights and misunderstandings. Jason felt overwhelmed by Sarah's need for closeness, and Belinda thought Jason was too distant.

Their relationship could have ended in disaster if not for a breakthrough realization: they both needed to learn the delicate dance of love and freedom. They discovered their rhythm by being honest with each other, setting limits, and respecting each other's needs. The dance was no longer a fight, but a peaceful duet in which each person helped the other without losing themselves in the process.

Each of us is on a different path to finding a balance between love and freedom. It requires self-awareness, communication, and a willingness to grow. It's not a place to go, but a journey, in which we learn and relearn as our relationships go through different stages.

• • • ● • ● • • ·

Cultivating Self-Compassion — Embracing the You Inside You

In the theater of life, self-compassion is like a kind and gentle director who guides you without judging you, knowing that mistakes and missed cues are all part of the show. It's about realizing that we're all human, fallible, and still deserving of love and acceptance.

Take Alan, a successful lawyer who is always critical of himself. His inner critic was relentless, pointing out every little error. That voice would get louder and hurt his self-esteem when he made mistakes in a relationship. Alan didn't start to see changes until he decided to turn down the volume on his inner critic and tune into a more compassionate channel.

He began to be kind, patient, and understanding toward himself, just as he would a close friend. This change had an impact on both his relationship with himself and the people around him. As he learned to show others the same compassion he had found for himself, his relationships got better.

Self-compassion isn't about ignoring or downplaying our flaws; it's about accepting them as part of the complex fabric that makes us who we are. It's about looking in the mirror and seeing not just the flaws but also the beauty, strength, and uniqueness that lies within.

How to Develop Self-compassion

What to Do:

Recognize What It Is and What It Isn't:

Recognize that self-compassion isn't about ignoring your flaws or avoiding hard truths. It's about realizing that you're human and that it's okay to make mistakes.

Practice Mindful Awareness:

Mindfulness is an essential component of self-compassion. Pay attention to what you say to yourself. Is it harsh and critical or kind and understanding? The key here is to observe without judging.

Use positive affirmations:

Write down kind things you can say to yourself when you're feeling down or stressed.

Embrace Common Humanity:

Recognize that you are not alone in your pain or mistakes and embrace common humanity. This is part of the human experience, and other people have felt like this before.

Seek Professional Help:

Professional therapists can sometimes help you build this important skill, especially if you find it difficult.

What Not to Do:

Don't Suppress or Deny Feelings:

It may be tempting to ignore difficult or painful feelings, but true self-compassion requires that you acknowledge them.

Don't Drown in Self-Criticism:

It's easy to become your own worst critic. Be aware of this tendency and actively combat it.

Don't isolate yourself:

Keep in mind that we're all in this together. If necessary, seek assistance from family, friends, or even a professional.

Examples

A Career Setback:

Consider a person who experienced a significant professional setback. Instead of beating himself up, he decides to take a step back and realize that failure is part of growing up. He takes time to think about the lessons he's learned, talks to himself with kindness and reaches out to friends who remind him that he's not the only one going through this.

Recovering from a Breakup:

A woman going through a painful breakup might get caught up in a cycle of blaming and shaming herself. However, by practicing self-compassion, she starts to treat herself with the same care she would give to a best friend. She gives herself permission to feel sad, does things she enjoys, and asks for help from people she cares about.

· · · ● · ● · · ·

Negative Self-Talk: A Deceptive Pitfall

Negative self-talk is the internal chatter that tends to criticize, doubt, or put ourselves down. It's like having a harsh critic living inside our heads, constantly judging our actions, appearance, and worth. This kind of self-talk is frequently present in our daily lives and can be very bad for our self-esteem and overall health.

Examples of Negative Self-Talk in Everyday Situations

During a Job Interview:

Imagine you're waiting for a job interview and a voice in your head starts to whisper, "You are not fit for this job. They'll see right through you." This kind of negative self-talk can make you feel more anxious and less sure of yourself, which could affect how well you perform.

After a Social Gathering:

You might think, "I talked too much, and I probably sounded stupid." This kind of self-criticism can change how you see social interactions and cause withdrawal or anxiety in social situations.

When Facing a New Challenge:

When trying something new, like a hobby or sport, you might find yourself thinking, "I'll never be good at this. Why even try?" This defeatist attitude can stop you from enjoying new things and can stop you from growing as a person.

In a Relationship:

If you're feeling insecure in a relationship, you might catch yourself thinking, "I'm not good enough for them. They deserve someone better." These thoughts can add unnecessary stress and tension to the relationship.

Why It's Simple to Fall for Negative Self-Talk

Because it can fit with our deepest fears and insecurities, negative self-talk often seems more real or true to us. Here's why it's so alluring:

It's Familiar:

Many of us have grown up with certain criticisms or judgments, and they become internalized.

It Makes You Feel Safe:

Sometimes, we use negative self-talk to get ready for disappointment. By putting ourselves first, we think we're softening the blow if things don't go well.

It Pretends to Be Realistic:

Negative self-talk often presents itself as "realistic" or "practical." It's easy to believe that it's a true reflection of our abilities or worth.

It's Reinforced by Culture:

Society often reinforces negative self-talk through media, social comparison, and even well-meaning advice from others.

• • • • • • • • • • •

The Oasis of Mindfulness and Holistic Practices

Mindfulness: The Practice of Being Here and Now

Mindfulness is the practice of being fully present in the moment, without judgment or distraction. It involves paying attention to your thoughts, feelings, and physical sensations without letting them control you. Here's how mindfulness helps the journey:

Emotional Stability:

Mindfulness encourages emotional stability by helping people recognize and accept their feelings without acting on impulse. It allows us to respond rather than react, which results in healthier relationships with ourselves and others.

Strengthening Connections:

Mindfulness encourages a closer relationship with oneself, which helps with self-awareness and compassion. It makes us more aware of our own needs and the needs of others, which strengthens our relationships.

How to Cultivate Mindfulness in the Context of Anxious Attachment

1- Understanding Anxious Attachment Triggers

Identify Your Triggers:

What situations or actions trigger your anxious feelings? Recognizing these things can make you more aware and help you respond in a more thoughtful way.

Watch Your Reactions:

Pay attention to how you act when these triggers occur. Do you become overly needy or maybe you pull away? Self-awareness can be fostered by observing without judgment.

2- Practice Mindful Breathing:

Focus on Breath:

When you're feeling anxious, pay attention to how you're breathing. Take a deep breath, hold it for a moment, and then slowly let it out. This easy exercise can bring calm and clarity.

Use it Anytime:

You can practice mindful breathing anywhere, at any time. Develop mindfulness as a daily habit.

3- Doing Mindful Activities:

Mindful Eating:

Pay full attention to the act of eating. Take note of the tastes, textures, and feelings.

Mindful Walking:

When walking, pay attention to each step, feeling your foot lift and touch the ground.

4- Cultivating Self-Compassion:

Speak Kindly to Yourself:

Replace critical self-talk with compassionate words. Treat yourself as you would a dear friend.

Embrace Imperfection:

Recognize that nobody is perfect, and it's okay to have flaws and make mistakes.

5- Creating Mindful Relationships:

Active Listening:

When conversing, focus fully on what the other person is saying without planning your response. This fosters deeper connections.

Express Feelings Mindfully:

Share your feelings and needs openly and without blame. It helps in building trust and understanding.

6- Maintaining a Mindfulness Journal:

Record Observations:

Write down your feelings, triggers, and observations regularly. You can learn more about yourself and keep track of your development by thinking about these.

7- Seeking Expert Advice if Necessary:

Therapists or Mindfulness Coaches:

Professional advice can be helpful if you find it difficult. Many therapists have received training in mindfulness techniques and can adapt them to your specific needs.

• • • • • • • • • •

Yoga: A Dance Between the Body and Mind

Yoga is more than just physical poses; it is a way to bring the mind, body, and spirit together in harmony. Yoga can have many positive effects:

Physical Well-being:

Yoga's asanas, or physical positions, encourage flexibility, strength, and balance. It promotes a more positive relationship with our bodies.

Emotional Healing:

Because yoga focuses on breath and movement, it can be a meditative experience that allows for emotional release and healing.

Mind-Body Connection:

Yoga's mindful approach encourages a stronger connection between the mind and body, which improves overall health.

• • • •●•●•• •

A Symphony of Wellness: Holistic Health

Holistic health looks at the whole person, not just the physical aspects but also the mental, emotional, and spiritual ones. There are many benefits to viewing health from this broader perspective:

Holistic health takes into account that each person is different. Healing plans are made specifically for each person based on their needs, preferences, and situation in life.

Places a Strong Emphasis on Prevention:

Holistic health focuses on prevention and long-term health rather than just treating symptoms.

Integrates Different Approaches:

Holistic health combines different modalities to provide complete care, including nutrition, herbal medicine, and psychotherapy.

Putting It All Together

Mindfulness, yoga, and holistic health are not stand-alone activities but rather interconnected parts of emotional and social well-being. They provide practical, approachable strategies for self-care, relationship enhancement, and navigating the intricate dynamics of anxious attachment.

It's not necessary to become a yogi or spend hours meditating to try out these practices. Even simple, everyday things like mindful breathing or eating a balanced diet can have a big effect.

We find rest and renewal, tools and insights, strength, and peace in the lush oasis of these practices. It's a journey of self-discovery, healing, and connection that anyone can take, no matter where they are in their own journey. It's a trip that's worth taking, and everyone is welcome.

· · · ● · ● · ● · ·

The Mirror of Self-Awareness

Let's dive into the world of self-awareness. Imagine looking into a mirror and seeing more than just your physical self. This is where the real work starts, where we learn to see ourselves clearly and honestly, not as a blurry image through a foggy lens.

A Clear View of Oneself

Life's pursuits and withdrawals are like tides; sometimes we move toward what we want and other times we move away from it. These movements may have their roots in our own self-deceptions or false beliefs about who we are and what we are capable of. Self-awareness is like a mirror, reflecting our true selves, free of illusions. Here's how to shine that mirror:

1. Recognizing the Pursuit-Withdrawal Dance:

Recognizing Patterns:

Do you keep pursuing relationships only to pull away when they get close? Or maybe you've noticed a tendency to avoid conflict, only to pursue it aggressively later. Breaking these patterns begins with awareness of them.

Understanding the Roots:

Investigating why these patterns happen can reveal underlying fears or beliefs that may be behind them. Maybe it's a fear of being rejected, or maybe it's a need to be in charge.

2. Fighting a Bad Self-Image:

Finding Negative Beliefs:

Do you think you're not good enough or loveable? It is crucial to recognize these deeply ingrained beliefs in order to challenge them.

Positive Self-Talk in its Place:

You can start to change the way you think by deliberately choosing words that are positive and encouraging. If you find yourself thinking, "I'll never find love," try saying, "I am worthy of love, and I'm open to finding it."

3. Stopping Lying to Yourself:

Recognize the Masks:

We often put on masks to protect ourselves, but these can lead to self-deception. Recognize when you're not being honest with yourself or with other people.

Embrace Authenticity:

Learning to be real, even when it makes you feel vulnerable, can help you make real connections and feel good about yourself.

4. Using a Journal to Reflect:

Keep a Self-Awareness Journal:

Note your thoughts, feelings, and observations regarding your actions and reactions. This written reflection can serve as a mirror, reflecting your inner self.

Review and reflect:

Reading your journal on a regular basis can help you keep track of your development and find areas that need more research.

5. If Help Is Needed, Seek Professional Advice:

Therapists or Counselors:

In order to understand intricate patterns of pursuit, withdrawal, or self-deception, professional guidance can be very helpful.

CHAPTER FOURTEEN

THERAPY AND PROFESSIONAL INTERVENTION

The landscape of healing and personal growth is vast, and within it are paths that can lead us to understanding, compassion, and transformation. There is no one-size-fits-all solution to the problem of anxious attachment. Some paths may resonate more than others, and it's up to you to find the one that does. In Chapter 6, we talked about cognitive behavioral therapy (CBT) and how it can help people with anxious attachment. This chapter examines various therapeutic modalities. Whether it's the vibrant colors of art or the comforting warmth of animal-assisted therapy, these techniques help people learn about themselves and get better. Let's look at the different kinds of therapy that go beyond traditional counseling and add their own special voices to the choir of recovery.

Art Therapy - Painting the Inner Landscape

Anxious attachment can feel like a jumble of feelings and ideas, like a picture with no shape or form. Art therapy gives you a chance to give that chaos shape, to paint your inner landscape and get to know its features.

Take Jake, a young man who was held back by his fear of abandonment. With a paintbrush in his hand and a wide range of colors in front of him, he began to paint his emotions. At first, his strokes were erratic, just like how he felt inside. As he worked with a skilled therapist, he started to see patterns in his paintings, echoes of past relationships, and the roots of his anxieties.

He didn't just paint his fears; he also started to reframe them, changing the patterns into new, more hopeful ones. Jake and his inner world communicated through the canvas during each session. He learned to recognize his fears, face them, and turn them into confidence and understanding.

Art therapy isn't about making works of art; it's about learning to control oneself. The canvas transforms into a mirror that reflects the soul during this process of self-exploration. It offers a gentle and expressive way to engage with deep-seated fears and desires, leading to profound insights and healing, for those who struggle with anxious attachment.

Animal-Assisted Therapy – Healing Through Bonding

Animals' unconditional love and acceptance can be a soothing balm in a world where human connections can feel scary or complicated, especially for those with anxious attachment. Animal-assisted therapy (AAT) uses this connection to promote growth, connection, and healing.

Meet Jacqueline, who was comforted by a therapy dog named Bella. Jacqueline had struggled with anxious attachment for years. She was always afraid of being rejected, so she never really let people in. The idea of traditional therapy was too scary, but Bella's wagging tail and friendly presence helped to build a bridge.

Jacqueline started to talk to Bella about her worries and fears in a safe place. She would talk to Bella, stroke her soft fur, and find comfort in the simple, accepting relationship they shared. Through AAT, she was able to start untying the knot of feelings that had been holding her back.

Bella wasn't there to judge or leave; she was a loyal friend and a listener without an agenda. Jacqueline was able to take those feelings into her relationships with other people thanks to this therapeutic bond, which also helped her understand what trust felt like.

But therapy involving animals goes beyond dogs. From horses to rabbits, different animals can help with healing. They offer a connection that isn't dangerous or scary, a relationship without the problems and worries that come with real-life interactions.

This therapy can be especially helpful for people who struggle with anxious attachment because it gives them a way to examine their attachment patterns without the pressure of being in a relationship right away. It can be a step toward deeper connections with other people, a way to ease into trust, and a way to learn about oneself in relation to others.

Group Therapy — The Power of Shared Experience

Imagine being in a room full of people who know what you're going through. They have experienced the pain of anxiety, the weight of constantly seeking approval, and the fear of abandonment that comes with anxious attachment. Welcome to the world of group therapy, a place where people can draw strength and find healing from their shared experiences.

Let's look more closely at Alan story. For most of his life, he felt alone because of his anxious attachment. Nobody seemed to understand what it was like to be in his position, and the loneliness was almost as bad as the anxiety.

Then, Alan found a group therapy program for people who were having trouble with attachment. He was suddenly no longer alone. People nodded in agreement and shared their stories, fears, and successes. Alan felt seen and understood in this community.

The realization that he wasn't alone was a powerful gift from group therapy. His problems were not unusual; they were common. This group experience started to break down the walls that his anxious attachment had built around him.

He could hear how other people dealt with similar problems, learn from them, and apply what he learned to his own life. Equally important, he could help others and turn his struggle into a way to understand and connect with them.

Group therapy has a growth-oriented dynamic. The group, which is led by an experienced therapist, creates a safe space where people can talk about their attachment patterns, learn from one another, and develop relationships that go beyond the therapy room.

Group therapy can be a game-changer for many people struggling with anxious attachment. It's a place where the intangible becomes real, where theories and concepts become stories and shared experiences. It's not just about healing yourself; it's also about growing as a community and realizing that we're all part of a bigger community, each on our own paths but never really alone.

As we come to the end of this chapter, we can see that the field of therapy is vast, varied, and full of chances. There isn't a single answer that works for everyone; instead, there are a lot of different ways to get what you want. The journey to overcoming anxious attachment is a very personal one, but it is also supported by a community of professionals. Each of these professionals has a different point of view, but they are all committed to helping people live healthier, more fulfilling lives.

CHAPTER FIFTEEN

SELF-CARE AND EMOTIONAL RESILIENCE

When life's problems are combined with the complexities of anxious attachment, it can feel like a maze. However, there is a way through this maze that leads to a safe place where healing, growth, and self-compassion can happen. In this chapter, we talk about that path and how important it is to practice self-care and emotional resilience. In these pages, you'll find the advice and tools you need to become your own best friend, which will help you feel calm and stable inside. Together, we'll learn about the art of loving yourself, which will give you the tools you need to succeed in your relationships and in your own life.

The Art of Self-Care: Loving Yourself First

Like our own distinct fingerprints, the field of self-care is vast and varied. It's a skill that, once mastered, can help you feel calm and sure of yourself even when things are going badly. And for those struggling with anxious attachment, this art has a deeper meaning.

Consider Maddie, a graphic designer from Atlanta who is in her mid-30s. Maddie's anxious attachment once threatened to consume her. It was a ghost that hung around in her relationships and made her doubt and feel uneasy. But then she learned how to take care of herself in a gentle way.

Maddie began by devoting a few minutes each day to meditation. Gradually, she added more ways to take care of herself, such as regular exercise, getting back into old hobbies, and, most importantly, setting boundaries. She didn't do these things by magic; rather, she chose to do them every day in order to build a caring relationship with herself.

The change was significant. As Maddie started to invest in herself, the anxious thoughts in her head started to fade away. Her relationships grew because she learned to value herself first, not because she clung to them.

The lesson is both simple and profound: It's not selfish to love yourself; it's essential. So how can we all be a little bit more like Maddie? How can we create our own masterpieces of self-care? Here are some routes:

Understanding Your Needs:

Figure out what really drives you. Is it a good book, a walk in the park, or maybe a creative hobby? Find your joy and make time for it.

Setting Limits:

Learn to say "no" when necessary. Protect your time, your energy, and your mental space.

Physical Wellness:

Invest in your body's health. Give your body the care it deserves, whether it's through nourishing food or a workout routine you enjoy.

There is no universally applicable model for self-care. It is a personal journey that changes over time. You give yourself a loving hug and promise to stay by your side, especially when the echoes of anxious attachment try to pull you away.

Some Ideas to Help You Practice Self-care

Here are some examples of different ways to take care of yourself that people, especially those who struggle with anxious attachment, might want to try:

Cultivating Inner Calm:

Set aside some time each day for meditation or mindfulness exercises. This practice helps you center yourself and stop worrying. It doesn't have to be an hour; even five minutes of focusing on your breath can make a big difference.

Physical Connection:

Taking part in physical activities that you enjoy can be a great way to take care of yourself. Moving your body, whether it's through yoga, running, dancing, or just taking a slow walk, helps release endorphins and makes you feel better.

Nutritional Nourishment:

Eating well is more than just providing your body with food; it's also a way to take care of yourself. It can be gratifying to prepare a meal that is both healthy and tasty. Making conscious decisions about what you eat and enjoying it with awareness can be satisfying, even if cooking isn't your thing.

Creative Activities:

If you enjoy making things, you might enjoy painting, writing, knitting, or doing other creative things. This can be a great way to express your feelings and get in touch with your inner self.

Spending time in nature:

Sometimes, a breath of fresh air and the sight of trees and flowers can do wonders for a mind that is feeling stressed. If you can, go for a walk in a nearby park, garden, or any other natural setting that speaks to you.

Building Connections:

While an anxious attachment may make relationships a little harder, it's important to keep in touch with friends and family who can help. Spend time with loved ones, do things together, or just have an open and honest conversation.

Personal Growth:

There are many ways to invest in one's own personal growth. It could be something as simple as reading a book that makes you think, going to a workshop, or picking up a new skill or hobby. The key is to choose something that fits with your interests and values.

Setting Boundaries:

This is a big one, especially for those with anxious attachment. Self-care includes learning to set clear and healthy boundaries in relationships. It could mean saying "no" when you need to or telling people what you need from them in a clear and assertive way.

Embracing Rest:

Because our lives are often busy, we tend to put rest last. But sometimes it can be very restorative to put sleep and relaxation first and to just "do nothing."

Resilience Training - Building Strength from Within

Life will always throw us a curve ball. Some days feel like a gentle breeze, while others feel like a violent storm. These storms may feel even more dangerous to those who suffer from anxious attachment because they pull at the very threads of our sense of safety and connection.

Resilience is about being able to weather those storms, not by avoiding them but by learning how to get through them. It's about realizing that we can do more than just survive; we can thrive, no matter what life throws at us.

In this section, we'll talk about how building resilience can help you deal with the hard things in life. We'll talk about how your anxious attachment affects how you react to stress and give you tips on how to develop a resilient mindset.

Building a Resilient Mindset

Knowing Your Triggers:

The first step in developing resilience is to figure out what makes you feel anxious. You can get ready for those times and develop coping mechanisms thanks to this information.

Embracing Failure as a Learning Opportunity:

Failure is not a loss; it is a lesson to be learned. By seeing failure as an opportunity to learn and grow, you can stop letting it get you down.

Creating a Support System:

Friends, family, therapists, and support groups can provide a safety net when you're feeling overwhelmed. Knowing that you have someone to lean on can make all the difference.

Implementing Mindfulness Practices:

As we've talked about in previous chapters, mindfulness can be a very effective tool for managing anxiety. Regular practice can improve emotional control and lessen impulsive behavior.

Celebrating Progress, Not Just Success:

Every step forward is something to be proud of. Focusing on progress can help you grow even more, whether it's by recognizing when you handled a stressful situation better than before or by recognizing relationship growth.

Resilience is not something you are born with or without. It's a skill that can be developed over time. It's about finding the inner strength to get back up after falling, learning from the experience, and moving forward with more wisdom and fortitude. Resilience can become a lighthouse that guides you through the stormy seas of life if you work at it and practice it. At the same time, you can develop an understanding and compassionate relationship with yourself.

CHAPTER SIXTEEN

PART IV: SUPPORT AND RESOURCES

SUPPORTING SOMEONE WITH ANXIOUS ATTACHMENT

As someone with anxious attachment who has been married to another anxiously attached person, I can attest to the complex dynamics that we share. My wife and I have been through the rough waters of love, trust, and understanding, learning to be the anchor for each other.

There were times when the storm seemed to never end, and we were almost sucked into the whirlpool of our shared fears. But through communication, empathy, and, when necessary, professional guidance, we made it. This chapter is more than just words on a page; it's a reflection of our own lives.

Guiding Lights for Friends and Family

Understanding Our World:

If you have a family member or friend who suffers from anxious attachment, you are probably aware of their need for reassurance, their fear of abandonment, and their desire for closeness. It's like a silent plea for connection, which people sometimes mistake for being clingy or needy. The first step toward empathy and help is to notice these signs.

Strategies for Communication:

Talking with someone who has anxious attachment requires a careful balance of honesty and kindness. Direct communication without judging or criticizing can help people understand each other better. Saying things like "I hear you" or "I'm here for you" can mean a lot.

Building trust and connection:

Trust is the foundation of any relationship, but it's even more important when dealing with anxious attachment. Being consistent, honest, and showing up when you say you will can help you get closer to someone. It's about being the steady light of love and support in the middle of their storm.

When Things Get Hard:

It's not always easy to help someone with an anxious attachment. There may be times when feelings run high, people don't understand each other, or old wounds start to hurt again. In these situations, the safe harbor can be patience, calm communication, and maybe even getting help from a professional.

In my own marriage, these ideas weren't just good to know, they were essential. There were nights when our worries loomed large, but we found comfort in the fact that we all wanted to learn and grow together. In the sections that follow, we'll keep talking about how hard it can be to help someone with anxious attachment, whether it's a friend, family member, or even ourselves.

Embracing the Echoes – Guidelines for the Anxiously Attached Dealing with Other Anxiously Attached Individuals

How can you, as an anxiously attached person, deal with people who have the same attachment style? Here is a path to understanding, acceptance, and growth.

1. Recognize the Similarities:

First and foremost, realizing that the other person is coming from a similar emotional place can be freeing. It's not a battle, but rather a shared experience. They experience the same fear, longing, and need for connection that you do.

2. Start a conversation:

Communication is the key to understanding. Share your emotions, your triggers, and what you want from the relationship. By letting them in, you make it easier for them to do the same, which strengthens your bond.

3. Establish Boundaries:

Anxious attachment can occasionally cause people to cross their own limits. Recognize what is appropriate for both parties and what is not. Setting clear and respectful boundaries can make a relationship healthier.

Relationships with two anxiously attached people can be intense and emotional. Patience with yourself and your partner can ease tension and create a loving atmosphere.

5. Get Professional Help If You Need It:

If things get too hard or conflicts keep happening, it can be a good idea to get professional help. Therapy can give you and your partner tools and techniques to deal with the worries you both have.

These rules have helped me in my own relationship. There were times when my wife and I felt like we were stuck in an endless cycle of anxiety and miscommunication. We got through it by drawing on what we had in common, being honest with each other, setting limits, and, when necessary, getting professional help.

A relationship between two anxiously attached people can grow into something beautiful with care, understanding, and love, just like a garden that needs tending and care. It's not an easy path, but it has a lot of potential for deep, meaningful connections. In the following section, we'll keep talking about anxious attachment and give you more tips, tricks, and reasons to hope for a happy relationship.

CHAPTER SEVENTEEN

RESOURCES AND FURTHER READING

You're never alone in the struggle to understand and get over anxious attachment. There is a wealth of information and help available, just waiting to be used. This chapter is a gateway to more information, professional help, and community support. It's not only a list of books to read, but also a map of places where empathy and understanding grow.

Books, Articles, and Websites - A Library at Your Fingertips

Books and articles can be your silent mentors through the labyrinth of anxious attachment. They give you information, viewpoints, and tools that you might not have otherwise. Here are some recommendations:

Books:

- "Attached" by Amir Levine and Rachel Heller: A seminal work on attachment theory that's both accessible and enlightening.

- "Insecure in Love: How Anxious Attachment Can Make You Feel Jealous, Needy, and Worried and What You Can Do About It" by Leslie Becker-Phelps

- "Wired for Love: How Understanding Your Partner's Brain and Attachment

Style Can Help You Defuse Conflict and Build a Secure Relationship" by Stan Tatkin

- "The Power of Attachment: How to Create Deep and Lasting Intimate Relationships" by Diane Poole Heller

- "Hold Me Tight: Seven Conversations for a Lifetime of Love" by Dr. Sue Johnson

- "Love Me, Don't Leave Me: Overcoming Fear of Abandonment and Building Lasting, Loving Relationships" by Michelle Skeen

Websites:

- AttachmentProject.com: A website dedicated to all things attachment, offering workshops, articles, and online sessions.

- Mindful.org: For those looking to explore mindfulness as a tool to manage anxiety, this website is a treasure trove of resources.

- The Gottman Institute: Renowned for its relationship research and resources, including those related to attachment.

- Mental Health America: Offers resources and support for various mental health conditions, including anxiety disorders.

- MindBodyGreen: A wellness site with numerous articles and courses on mindful living, relationships, and mental health.

Support Groups:

- Anxious Attachment Support Group: Various local and online groups focus on connecting people with similar experiences.

- Meetup.com: A platform where you can find local meetups related to mental health and personal growth.

Counseling Services:

- PsychologyToday.com: A directory for therapists specializing in attachment issues.

- Talkspace: An online therapy platform that connects you with licensed therapists from the comfort of your home.

CHAPTER EIGHTEEN

INTERACTIVE ELEMENTS

Worksheets – A Personal Exploration

Anxious Attachment Self-Assessment: Identifying Patterns, Triggers, and Behaviors

This self-assessment will help you explore your attachment patterns, particularly those related to anxious attachment. As you go through the statements below, reflect on how they relate to your feelings, thoughts, and behaviors in relationships. This is not a diagnostic tool but a guide to understanding yourself better.

Instructions

1. **Read each statement carefully.**

2. **Rate how true each statement is for you on a scale from 0 to 4.**

   - 0 = Not true at all

   - 1 = Rarely true

   - 2 = Sometimes true

- ○ 3 = Often true

- ○ 4 = Always true

3. **Total your score at the end.**

Assessment Statements

1. I often worry that my partner doesn't really love me.

2. I feel a strong need to be close to my partner and become anxious if I'm not.

3. I find it difficult to trust others completely.

4. I become preoccupied with my relationships and struggle to focus on other things.

5. When I feel unsure about a relationship, I need constant reassurance.

6. My fear of rejection influences my actions and decisions in relationships.

7. I feel uncomfortable when someone wants to be emotionally close to me.

8. I have experienced intense jealousy in relationships.

9. I struggle to express my needs and feelings openly.

10. I often overanalyze my partner's words and actions for hidden meanings.

Scoring Guide

- **0-10**: Low anxious attachment tendencies. Your responses indicate that anxious attachment is not a predominant pattern for you.

- **11-20**: Mild anxious attachment tendencies. You may have some behaviors or thoughts associated with anxious attachment, but they don't define your relational style.

- **21-30**: Moderate anxious attachment tendencies. Anxious attachment patterns appear to be a noticeable part of your relational dynamic. Exploring these with professional guidance may be beneficial.

- **31-40**: High anxious attachment tendencies. Your responses suggest that anxious attachment is a significant aspect of your relationships. Seeking professional help to understand and work on these patterns may be highly valuable.

Reflective Questions (Optional)

- What patterns or behaviors stood out to you as you took this assessment?

- Are there specific relationships or situations where you notice these tendencies more?

- How might these patterns impact your current and future relationships?

- What steps could you take to address the triggers or behaviors you've identified?

• • • ● • ● • ● • •

Relationship Mapping: Exploring Dynamics and Attachment Styles in Various Relationships

Introduction

Relationship Mapping is an exercise that helps you visually represent and understand the dynamics of your relationships with different people in your life. By recognizing the attachment styles that govern these relationships, you can gain insights into patterns, challenges, and areas for growth.

Instructions

1. **List Key Relationships**: Write down the names of significant people in your life such as family, friends, romantic partners, colleagues, etc.

2. **Identify Your Feelings & Behaviors**: Next to each name, jot down how you feel about this person and how you behave around them. Be honest and specific.

3. **Determine Attachment Styles**: Reflect on each relationship and determine the attachment style that best describes it (secure, anxious, avoidant, etc.). You may refer back to the descriptions of these styles from previous chapters.

4. **Draw Connections & Patterns**: Create a visual map by connecting relationships that share similar dynamics or styles. Use lines, colors, or symbols to represent different themes.

5. **Reflect**: Consider the following reflective questions.

Reflective Questions

- **What patterns or themes emerge from your map?** Are there certain attachment styles that predominate in specific areas of your life?

- **How do different attachment styles influence your interactions?** Think about how an anxious attachment might affect your relationship with a particular person versus a secure attachment.

- **What surprises you about your map?** Are there unexpected insights or contradictions?

- **How might understanding these dynamics support your growth?** Consider the steps you could take to foster healthier connections or shift problematic patterns.

Example

- **Person**: Jessica (friend)

- **Feelings & Behaviors**: Comfortable, supportive, sometimes anxious about pleasing her

- **Attachment Style**: Mostly secure, occasional anxious tendencies

- **Connection to Other Relationships**: Similar dynamic with sibling

Relationship Mapping is more than just an analytical tool; it's a means of self-discovery. By visually representing and exploring the dynamics of various relationships, you uncover layers of understanding about yourself and how you connect with others. It may reveal imbalances, dependencies, or strengths that you weren't aware of, and provide a pathway toward more fulfilling and balanced relationships.

• • • ● • ● • ● • • •

Goal Setting: Crafting Personalized Plans to Address Anxious Attachment

Introduction

Anxious attachment can manifest in various ways in our lives, affecting relationships, self-esteem, and overall well-being. Recognizing the patterns is the first step; the next is setting concrete, actionable goals to work on these areas. Goal setting in this context isn't merely about setting targets but crafting a personalized roadmap toward emotional growth and healthier relationships.

Instructions

1. **Identify Your Needs**: What aspects of anxious attachment are most prominent in your life? Is it a fear of abandonment, clinginess, or something else? Write down what resonates with you.

2. **Set Specific Goals**: Based on your needs, set clear and specific goals. Make them measurable, achievable, relevant, and time-bound (SMART goals).

   - Example: "I will spend 15 minutes daily practicing mindfulness to reduce anxiety for the next 30 days."

3. **Create Action Steps**: Break down the goals into smaller, manageable action steps. Outline what you will do, how often, and how you'll know you're making progress.

4. **Identify Support**: Who or what can support you in this journey? Whether it's a friend, family member, or a professional, ensure you have the support structure you need.

5. **Monitor Progress**: Regularly check in with yourself to see how you're progressing towards your goals. Adjust as necessary.

6. **Celebrate Successes**: Even small victories are worth celebrating. Acknowledge

and reward yourself for progress.

Reflective Questions

- **Why are these goals important to you?** Understanding the 'why' can be a powerful motivator.

- **What challenges do you anticipate?** Foreseeing obstacles allows you to prepare for them.

- **How will you maintain motivation?** Think about strategies to keep yourself engaged and committed.

- **What will success look like?** Visualize what achieving these goals will mean for you.

Example

- **Need**: Fear of abandonment

- **Goal**: "I will communicate my feelings openly with my partner instead of withdrawing, at least once a week for the next two months."

- **Action Steps**: Practice communication techniques, schedule regular check-ins, journal about experiences

- **Support**: Partner's cooperation, therapist guidance

The journey of overcoming anxious attachment is highly personal, and the goals and plans you set should reflect your unique situation and needs. By focusing on what matters most to you, breaking it down into actionable steps, and continually reflecting and adjusting, you can turn insights into transformative actions. Remember, progress takes time, and self-compassion is a vital companion in this process.

• • • ● • ● • • •

Quizzes - Assessing and Understanding

What's Your Attachment Style?

Discover your primary attachment style by answering the following questions as honestly as possible. Your attachment style affects how you relate to others, especially in close relationships, and understanding it can pave the way to more satisfying connections.

Instructions

- Read each statement and choose the option that best reflects your feelings or behaviors in close relationships.

- Keep track of your answers.

Questions

1. **When my partner is away, I often feel:**

    o a. Anxious and worried.

    o b. Comfortable, knowing they will return.

    o c. Disinterested or indifferent.

    o d. Slightly uneasy but generally okay.

2. **In a relationship, I often find myself:**

    o a. Needing reassurance and fearing rejection.

    o b. Trusting and content.

    o c. Avoiding closeness and emotional connection.

    o d. Wanting closeness but fearing dependence.

3. **When faced with a problem in a relationship, my instinct is to:**

  ○ a. Cling and seek constant reassurance.

  ○ b. Communicate openly and work through it together.

  ○ c. Withdraw or dismiss the issue.

  ○ d. Struggle between wanting to address it and fearing conflict.

4. **I describe my relationship with my parents or caregivers as:**

  ○ a. Inconsistent, sometimes nurturing, sometimes neglectful.

  ○ b. Warm, supportive, and nurturing.

  ○ c. Distant and unemotional.

  ○ d. A mix of closeness and distance.

5. **When someone I'm close to needs space, I feel:**

  ○ a. Extremely anxious and abandoned.

  ○ b. Supportive of their need while maintaining my sense of self.

  ○ c. Relieved and prefer my own space as well.

  ○ d. Conflicted, both understanding and anxious.

Scoring Guide

- **Mostly As**: Anxious Attachment - You often worry about rejection and seek constant reassurance from loved ones.

- **Mostly Bs**: Secure Attachment - You feel comfortable in relationships and trust in your connections.

- **Mostly Cs**: Avoidant Attachment - You tend to keep an emotional distance and may struggle with intimacy.

- **Mostly Ds**: Disorganized Attachment - You may feel torn between wanting closeness and fearing dependence.

Understanding your attachment style is a vital step in recognizing patterns and behaviors in relationships. It's not a static label but rather a dynamic aspect of who you are that can be nurtured and evolved. Whether you identify with Anxious, Secure, Avoidant, or Disorganized Attachment, embracing self-awareness is the beginning of a transformative journey.

• • • ● • ● • • •

Relationship Dynamics Quiz: Anxious Attachment in Action

Understanding how anxious attachment influences your relationship dynamics can help you recognize patterns, create awareness, and nurture healthier connections. Take this quiz to assess how anxious attachment might manifest in your relationships.

Instructions

- Read each scenario and choose the option that best reflects your reaction or feelings.
- Keep track of your answers.

Questions

1. **Your partner is late for a dinner date without informing you. Your reaction is:**

   - a. Panic, fear they have abandoned you.
   - b. Mild irritation, but trust they have a reason.
   - c. Indifference, you barely notice their lateness.
   - d. A mix of concern and understanding.

2. **A friend hasn't replied to your text for a day. You think:**

   - a. They must be mad at me or losing interest in our friendship.
   - b. They're probably busy and will get back to me when they can.
   - c. It's not a big deal, I don't need constant communication.
   - d. I'm curious but will wait to see if anything's wrong.

3. **In a relationship, your typical pattern of communication is:**

- a. Constantly checking in, needing reassurance.

- b. Regular, balanced communication.

- c. Infrequent and distant.

- d. Sometimes too much, sometimes too little, fluctuating.

4. **A family member is distant at a gathering. You feel:**

- a. Personally responsible and anxious about what you might have done wrong.

- b. Curious but patient, giving them space.

- c. Unaffected, focusing on other things.

- d. Concerned but cautious about overreacting.

5. **Your boss gives you a neutral comment on your work. You interpret it as:**

- a. A sign of dissatisfaction, fearing job loss.

- b. Objective feedback, feeling secure in your performance.

- c. Unimportant, disregarding their opinion.

- d. Uncertain, torn between taking it positively or negatively.

Scoring Guide

- **Mostly As**: Anxious Dynamics - You often react with anxiety and fear in relationships, seeking reassurance.

- **Mostly Bs**: Balanced Dynamics - You approach relationships with trust and understanding.

- **Mostly Cs**: Distant Dynamics - You may keep an emotional distance, avoiding deep connections.

- **Mostly Ds**: Mixed Dynamics - Your reactions fluctuate, sometimes mirroring anxious attachment, other times showing balance or distance.

Conclusion

Recognizing how anxious attachment may shape your relationships is the first step towards growth. If you find that anxious dynamics resonate with you, exploring these patterns with a mental health professional or through self-help materials can support positive change. Relationships are a complex dance, and understanding your unique rhythm can lead to more fulfilling connections.

Note: This quiz is designed to provide insights and is not a definitive assessment. Consult with a mental health professional if you seek further exploration of your relationship dynamics and attachment style.

• • • ● ● • ● ● • • •

Exercises - A Path to Growth

Mindfulness Exercises: Finding Presence in the Now

The journey towards understanding and working with anxious attachment is deeply personal. Mindfulness can be a powerful tool in this process. Below, you'll find exercises to help you cultivate awareness, presence, and compassion for yourself.

Exercise 1: Mindful Breathing

Objective: To anchor yourself in the present moment and alleviate anxiety.

1. Find a comfortable and quiet spot.

2. Close your eyes or soften your gaze, focusing on your breath.

3. Breathe in deeply through your nose, noticing the sensation in your nostrils, chest, and belly.

4. Exhale slowly through your mouth, paying attention to the sensation as your breath leaves your body.

5. Repeat for 5-10 minutes, gently bringing your mind back to your breath if it wanders.

Exercise 2: Body Scan Meditation

Objective: To connect with your physical sensations and recognize any areas of tension.

1. Lie down or sit in a comfortable position.

2. Starting at your toes, focus on each part of your body, moving upward.

3. Notice sensations, temperature, and any tension or relaxation.

4. If you find tension, breathe into that area, imagining it releasing as you exhale.

5. Continue to scan your entire body, taking 10-20 minutes.

Exercise 3: Mindful Observation

Objective: To cultivate presence and connection to your surroundings.

1. Choose an object or scene, like a flower, painting, or window view.

2. Spend 5 minutes observing it, noticing details like color, texture, shape, and movement.

3. If your mind wanders, gently return to your observation, embracing curiosity.

Exercise 4: Compassionate Self-Talk

Objective: To develop a compassionate inner dialogue, especially during moments of anxiety.

1. Think of a situation that triggers anxious attachment feelings.

2. Imagine a wise and compassionate friend giving you advice and support.

3. Write down or speak aloud what they would say, using gentle and reassuring words.

4. Internalize this compassionate voice and call upon it when needed.

These exercises aim to support your journey toward greater self-awareness and presence. Mindfulness is a skill, and it takes practice and patience. By regularly engaging in these exercises, you can cultivate a deeper understanding of yourself and your anxious attachment patterns. This inner connection can lead to more fulfilling and balanced relationships, allowing you to navigate life's twists and turns with grace and wisdom.

Note: Mindfulness practices are not a substitute for professional mental health care if needed. Consider seeking support from a therapist or counselor if you find that anxious attachment is significantly impacting your life.

• • • ● • ● • • •

Communication Exercises: Speaking from the Heart

When anxious attachment takes the stage, communication can become clouded by fear, uncertainty, and misinterpretation. These exercises are designed to sharpen your ability to express yourself clearly and compassionately, understanding the needs and feelings of both parties involved.

Exercise 1: The "I Feel" Statement

Objective: To express feelings and needs without blaming or criticizing.

1. Choose a situation where communication felt challenging.

2. Practice framing your feelings using "I feel [emotion] when [situation] because [reason]. What I need is [need]."

3. Repeat with different scenarios, noticing how it changes the energy of the conversation.

Exercise 2: Role-Playing Difficult Conversations

Objective: To practice navigating tough conversations with empathy and clarity.

1. Choose a partner (friend, family, therapist) to role-play with.

2. Select a real or imagined scenario involving anxious attachment.

3. Take turns playing both roles, experimenting with different responses and emotions.

4. Afterward, discuss what felt effective, empathetic, and true to your feelings.

Exercise 3: Active Listening Practice

Objective: To cultivate the skill of truly hearing and understanding another's perspective.

1. Partner with someone and choose a topic.

2. One person speaks for 2-3 minutes while the other listens without interruption.

3. The listener then reflects back what they heard without judgment or advice.

4. Switch roles and repeat, focusing on empathy and validation.

Exercise 4: The Pause Technique

Objective: To develop awareness and control over reactive communication patterns.

1. Notice when you feel triggered in a conversation.

2. Pause before responding, taking a deep breath, or even asking for time if needed.

3. Reflect on what you need to say and how best to express it.

4. Practice this in daily interactions, observing how it transforms your communication style.

Anxious attachment can create barriers in communication, but with intention and practice, those barriers can be overcome. These exercises are a roadmap to more authentic, compassionate, and effective communication. By putting them into practice, you're not only working on personal growth but also cultivating healthier, more fulfilling relationships. The path may be winding, but the destination is worth the journey.

Remember, these exercises may bring up emotions, and it's normal to feel vulnerable. If you find that you need further support, don't hesitate to reach out to a mental health professional or counselor who specializes in attachment issues. The goal is to grow, not to go it alone.

• • • ● ●• ● • • ••

Emotional Regulation Techniques: Steering the Ship of Feelings

Anxious attachment can often lead to intense emotional reactions. Whether it's fear, anger, sadness, or overwhelm, these feelings can take over, making it hard to navigate relationships and life itself. Emotional regulation is like learning to steer a ship through stormy seas; it requires skill, practice, and patience. The following techniques are designed to help you learn to manage and balance emotions related to anxious attachment.

Technique 1: Emotional Awareness Journaling

Objective: To identify triggers and patterns in your emotional reactions.

1. Keep a daily journal of situations where anxious attachment triggers intense emotions.

2. Note the event, feelings, thoughts, body sensations, and actions taken.

3. Reflect on patterns and insights that arise, helping to build awareness and understanding.

Technique 2: Mindful Breathing and Grounding

Objective: To calm the nervous system and create space for balanced responses.

1. Practice taking slow, deep breaths, focusing on the sensation of air entering and leaving your lungs.

2. If you feel overwhelmed, ground yourself by noticing five things you can see, four things you can touch, three things you can hear, two things you can smell, and one thing you can taste.

3. Use these techniques as needed to soothe anxiety and bring yourself back to the present moment.

Technique 3: Creating an Emotional Safety Plan

Objective: To develop a personalized toolkit for managing emotional spikes.

1. Identify specific emotions that arise with anxious attachment.

2. List healthy coping strategies for each emotion, such as talking to a friend, going for a walk, or practicing a hobby.

3. Refer to this plan when emotions escalate, applying the strategies that feel most appropriate.

Technique 4: Self-Compassion Practice

Objective: To foster kindness and understanding toward oneself.

1. Acknowledge emotions without judgment, recognizing that feelings are natural and human.

2. Offer yourself comforting words, as you would to a dear friend in distress.

3. Practice self-compassion meditations or repeat affirmations that resonate with your experience.

Technique 5: Seek Professional Support

Objective: To get personalized assistance in developing emotional regulation skills.

1. Consider therapy or support groups that focus on attachment issues.

2. Collaborate with a mental health professional to create strategies tailored to your unique situation.

3. Utilize therapy as a safe space to explore, practice, and refine these techniques under expert guidance.

Emotional regulation doesn't mean suppressing or denying feelings. Instead, it's about learning to navigate them with wisdom, grace, and resilience. By applying these techniques, you can create a more balanced and empowered relationship with yourself and others, turning anxious attachment's turbulent waters into a journey of growth and healing.

• • • ● • ● • • ·

Tools for Support Systems

Supporting Someone with Anxious Attachment: Lighting the Pathway Together

Understanding Anxious Attachment

Anxious attachment often stems from inconsistent caregiving in childhood. Individuals with this attachment style may have heightened anxieties around relationships, fearing abandonment or rejection. They may seek constant reassurance and may react intensely to perceived slights or indifference.

Role-Playing Scenario 1: Offering Reassurance

Situation: Your partner with anxious attachment is feeling insecure about your relationship after a minor disagreement.

- **You**: "I understand that our disagreement earlier has left you feeling unsure. I want you to know that I value our relationship and I'm committed to working through this with you. Let's talk about what's bothering you."

- **Partner**: Response

- **You**: Offer empathy, reassurance, and an actionable plan to address the concerns.

Role-Playing Scenario 2: Setting Boundaries

Situation: A friend with anxious attachment is calling frequently, seeking validation and reassurance, impacting your personal time.

- **You**: "I care about you and our friendship, but I need to set some boundaries around our communication. Can we find a time that works for both of us to catch up?"

- **Friend**: Response

- **You**: Acknowledge feelings, clarify boundaries, and suggest alternative support options if needed.

Role-Playing Scenario 3: Encouraging Professional Support

Situation: A family member's anxious attachment behaviors are escalating, affecting their well-being and relationships.

- **You**: "I've noticed you've been struggling a lot with anxiety in your relationships lately. Have you considered speaking to a mental health professional? I can help you find someone if you like."

- **Family Member**: Response

- **You**: Offer understanding, information, and assistance without pushing or judging.

Key Principles in Supporting Someone with Anxious Attachment:

- **Empathize**: Show understanding and compassion for their feelings and fears.

- **Communicate Clearly**: Use open and honest communication, clarifying intentions and expectations.

- **Maintain Boundaries**: While offering support, don't lose sight of your own needs and boundaries.

- **Encourage Growth**: Support their personal growth, including suggesting professional help if necessary.

- **Be Patient and Consistent**: Building trust takes time and consistent behavior.

Supporting someone with anxious attachment is a nuanced journey that requires empathy, clear communication, and patience. These role-playing scenarios are just a beginning; real-life interactions may be more complex and will require ongoing learning and growth. The key lies in a shared commitment to understanding and a willingness to walk this path together, lighting the way with compassion and wisdom.

· • • ● · ● • • ·

Developing Empathy and Understanding: Bridging Hearts and Minds

Empathy and understanding are foundational elements in human connection. They can transform relationships, especially when dealing with anxious attachment. Below are exercises to help cultivate these crucial skills.

Exercise 1: The Empathy Journal

Objective: To understand the feelings and thoughts of others by reflecting on their experiences.
Instructions:

1. Choose a person you interacted with today.

2. Write a short description of an interaction you had with them.

3. Imagine what they might have been feeling and thinking during this interaction.

4. Reflect on how your actions might have influenced their feelings.

5. Write about how this exercise affects your understanding of that person.

Exercise 2: The Compassionate Listener

Objective: To practice active and compassionate listening without judgment or immediate advice.
Instructions:

1. Pair up with a partner and choose who will speak first.

2. The speaker shares a personal experience or concern.

3. The listener focuses on fully understanding the speaker, reflecting feelings, and asking open-ended questions.

4. Switch roles and repeat.

5. Discuss how it felt to be truly listened to and to listen with compassion.

Exercise 3: Walking in Their Shoes

Objective: To deepen empathy by imagining yourself in another person's situation.
Instructions:

1. Think of someone you know who is going through a challenging time, such as dealing with anxious attachment.

2. Reflect on their daily life, struggles, fears, and needs.

3. Write a letter to yourself from their perspective, explaining their feelings and asking for what they need from you.

4. Consider how this exercise shifts your perspective and how you can support them.

Exercise 4: The Connection Circle

Objective: To foster understanding and connection within a group setting.
Instructions:

1. Gather a group of friends or family members.

2. Everyone writes down a personal challenge or feeling on a piece of paper.

3. Place the papers in a bowl, and each person draws one.

4. Read the challenges aloud, and each person shares how they might feel if they were facing that challenge.

5. Discuss as a group how understanding each other's struggles can strengthen connections.

Developing empathy and understanding is a lifelong journey. These exercises are not just tools for building skills; they are pathways to deeper connections, richer relationships, and a more compassionate world. By seeking to understand the world through the eyes of others, we bridge hearts and minds, creating a space where empathy blossoms and anxious attachment finds comfort and care.

CONCLUSION: CONTINUING THE JOURNEY OF CONNECTION AND GROWTH

As we come to the end of this exploration into the complicated world of anxious attachment, it's a good idea to take a moment to think about the journey we've been on together. Through the pages of this book, we've gone through the twists and turns of relationships, emotions, self-awareness, and personal growth.

We began by learning a lot about anxious attachment, including where it comes from, what makes it worse, and what kinds of behaviors it can cause. It wasn't just a study of patterns and reactions; it also revealed human emotions and the connection that unites us all.

In the chapters that followed, we took a trip through the landscapes of relationships, whether they were between parents and children, romantic partners, or coworkers. We learned how important it is to understand our attachment styles and how much of an impact they can have on our interactions.

Understanding was only the beginning of our search. We discussed the tools and techniques required to cultivate self-compassion, mindfulness, and emotional resilience. We talked about therapies, coping mechanisms, and practical steps to take to deal with the difficulties that come with anxious attachment.

We also talked about the supportive roles we can play for our friends, family, and even ourselves. The resources and interactive parts of this book are meant to help you on this personal journey by giving you insights and exercises to help you connect with people more deeply.

Remember that the journey doesn't end here as we end this chapter. Growth is a process that never ends, and knowing your attachment style is just the beginning. You have the knowledge, tools, and hopeful stories you need to keep exploring, learning, and connecting.

Your path to emotional balance and healthy relationships is unique to you. Accept it with a sense of wonder, courage, and compassion. Keep looking, practicing, and changing. Above all, remember that you are not alone on this journey. We are all connected in our struggles, our growth, and our search for real, meaningful relationships.

I appreciate you letting me be a part of your journey. Here's to being our true selves, making connections that matter, and building a life that is full of love, understanding, and fulfillment.

Jeff

PLEASE CONSIDER LEAVING A REVIEW

Hello there!

As an author, I know just how important reviews are for getting the word out about my work. When readers leave a review on Amazon or any other book stores, it helps others discover my book and decide whether it's right for them.

Plus, it gives me valuable feedback on what readers enjoyed and what they didn't.

So if you've read my book and enjoyed it (or even if you didn't!), I would really appreciate it if you took a moment to leave a review on Amazon. It doesn't have to be long or complicated - just a few words about what you thought of the book would be incredibly helpful.

Thank you so much for your support!

Jeff

ALSO BY JEFFREY C. CHAPMAN

Adulting Hard for Young Men

• • • ● • ● • • •

Adulting Hard for Young Women

• • • ● • ● • • •

Adulting Hard After College

• • • ● • ● • • •

Adulting Hard in Your Late Twenties and Thirties

• • • ● • ● • • •

Adulting Hard For Couples

. . . ●.●●. ●.

Adulting Hard for New Parents

. . ●.● ●. ●.

Adulting Hard as an Introvert or Highly Sensitive Person

• • • • • • • • • •

Adulting Hard and Laughing Harder

• • • • • • • • • •

101 Questions to Ask Before You Get Engaged

Made in the USA
Columbia, SC
26 January 2024

30966743R00096